ENERGY FOR THE FUTURE AND GLOBAL WARMING

WATER POWER

By Andrew Solway

Consultant: Suzy Gazlay, M.A., science curriculum resource teacher

Gareth Stevens
Publishing

Please visit our web site at: www.garethstevens.com
For a free color catalog describing Gareth Stevens Publishing's
list of high-quality books, call 1-800-542-2595 (USA)
or 1-800-387-3178 (Canada).

Library of Congress Cataloging-in-Publication Data

Solway, Andrew.
    Water power / Andrew Solway.
       p. cm. — (Energy for the future and global warming)
    Includes index.
    ISBN: 978-0-8368-8404-3 (lib. bdg.)
    ISBN: 978-0-8368-8413-5 (softcover)
    1. Water power—Juvenile literature. I. Title.
  TC146.S65   2008
  621.31'2134—dc22   2007008754

This edition first published in 2008 by
Gareth Stevens Publishing
A Weekly Reader® Company
1 Reader's Digest Road
Pleasantville, NY 10570-7000 USA

Produced by Discovery Books
Editors: Geoff Barker and Sabrina Crewe
Designer: Keith Williams
Photo researcher: Rachel Tisdale
Illustrations: Stefan Chabluk

Gareth Stevens editor: Carol Ryback
Gareth Stevens art direction and design: Tammy West
Gareth Stevens production: Jessica Yanke

Photo credits: Bureau of Reclamation: cover, title page. CIV/DOD: / Gary Nichol 7.
istockphoto.com: / 10; / Geoff Kuchera 11; / Jack Morris 15; / Matej Michelizza 20;
/ Eric Foltz 29. U.S. Department of Agriculture: / 18. CORBIS: / Yann Arthus-Bertrand
24. Enwave Energy Corporation: / 26.

Printed in the United States of America

1 2 3 4 5 6 7 8 9 11 10 09 08 07

CONTENTS

Cover image: Hoover Dam, on the Nevada-Arizona border,
was completed in 1936. The dam first produced electricity on October
26, 1936.

Words in **boldface** appear in the glossary or in the "Key Words"
boxes within the chapters.

CHAPTER ONE
ENERGY AND GLOBAL WARMING

Every day, the world needs more energy to keep things going. There are two main reasons for this increase in demand. First, there are more people in the world each day. Today, there are almost three times as many people as there were fifty years ago.

The second reason is that nations use more energy as they develop. The standard of living is changing in **developing nations**. People build more factories and buy more cars. They get heating for their homes. To power these things, people use more fuel and more electricity.

HOW ENERGY USE IS GROWING

People who live in countries in North America and Europe are rich compared to most of the rest of the world. They already use a lot of energy in their daily lives. Many countries on other continents are rapidly developing, however. Energy use in Asian countries — especially in China — is increasing by great amounts annually. Other countries in the Mideast, Africa, and South America will soon require their share of energy resources. By 2030, the world will need about twice as much fuel as in 2005.

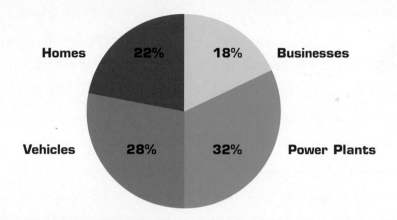

Homes 22% 18% Businesses

Vehicles 28% 32% Power Plants

This chart shows energy use in the United States. It shows how much was used by homes, businesses, power plants, and vehicles.

Fossil fuels

Today, we get most of our energy by burning coal, oil, or natural gas. These fuels are known as **fossil fuels**. They formed from the remains of plants or animals that lived millions of years ago.

We use fossil fuels in several ways. Most **power plants** make electricity by burning fossil fuels. Cars, ships, and airplanes all run on gasoline, diesel, or other fuels made from oil.

In the past one hundred years, we have used up large amounts of the world's supply, or **reserves**, of fossil fuels. There are still huge reserves in the ground. But fossil fuels are not renewable. They cannot be replaced. Even energy experts do not know exactly how long fossil fuels will last. Coal, oil, and natural gas may run out at different times over the next three hundred years.

Pollution from fossil fuels

Scientists have shown that burning fossil fuels is polluting Earth. Pollution happens when harmful substances are put into the land, air, or water.

When fossil fuels burn, they produce **emissions** — waste gases that cause pollution. Coal is the fossil fuel that makes the most pollution. Oil, which we burn for heat and to run vehicles, also causes a lot of pollution. Pollution from fossil fuels can cause smog (a thick, dirty kind of fog). Fossil fuel emissions also cause acid rain, sleet, and snow. Scientists group all these under the term "acid rain." It can kill fish and damage trees and buildings.

Global warming

Burning fossil fuels also give off **greenhouse gases**, such as carbon dioxide and water vapor. Greenhouse gases trap heat in the atmosphere. They keep Earth warm enough for living things to exist. When too much heat is trapped, Earth gets warmer than usual.

The amounts of greenhouse gases in the air have increased in the last one hundred years. Scientists believe this increase is causing Earth to get warmer. This warming changes worldwide weather patterns, or the climate. This climate change is called **global warming**.

Renewable and clean

People are finding ways to reduce pollution and help slow global warming. If we use fewer fossil fuels, we will release less carbon dioxide

EFFECTS OF GLOBAL WARMING

Global warming is affecting the whole planet. At the North and South Poles, global warming is causing large ice sheets to melt. Water from the melted ice flows into the oceans and causes worldwide sea levels to rise. As ocean levels rise, coastal lands will flood. Global warming causes other changes as well. Some areas become too wet, while others becme too dry. As temperatures rise, certain regions may become deserts. Some regions now used for farming may become too hot and dry to grow crops.

In 2005, Hurricane Katrina flooded large portions of New Orleans, Louisiana. Scientists predict that extreme weather events, such as hurricanes, will become more common as global warming increases.

CHAPTER TWO

AN ANCIENT SOURCE OF POWER

Water power, or **hydropower**, has been around for a long time. More than two thousand years ago, people were using water to work machinery. They did this with **waterwheels** — wheels turned by the force of falling or running water. The first waterwheels may have been invented in the Middle East, India, or China. Many societies used them, including the ancient Greeks and Romans.

Types of waterwheel

Early waterwheels were set horizontally (flat) in the water. The current of the river or stream turned the wheel. It was connected to a large stone for grinding corn.

The force of falling water turns an overshot waterwheel and generates power. Water power is a free, renewable resource.

As a waterwheel turned, it turned the grindstone. By about 100 A.D., another kind of waterwheel was being used. This wheel was vertical (upright). Upright wheels produced more power.

Upright waterwheels can have either an overshot or an undershot style. Water falling from above turns an overshot wheel. This design is more **efficient** (produces more power) than an undershot wheel, which turns as flowing water pushes against the bottom of the wheel.

Water flowing against the bottom of the wheel turns an undershot waterwheel. Many waterwheels that once generated power are now used only for decoration.

Using waterwheels

Throughout history, waterwheels have been used in many ways. The Chinese used them

CRAGSIDE HOUSE

In 1870, eleven years before the first power plant was built, Cragside House in Godalming, Britain, became the first building in the world to have electricity. The electricity was used to power arc lights (a kind of very bright electric light first made in the early 1800s). Cragside House used arc lights because the lightbulb had not yet been invented! Thomas Edison patented the lightbulb in 1879.

to power hammers hundreds of years ago. The hammers crushed rocks to make a powder used in porcelain. Arab peoples were skillful at harnessing hydropower. Waterwheels ground corn for flour, crushed sugar beets to make sugar, and pounded wood pulp to make paper. Europeans used waterwheels for those purposes — and to saw wood. Miners used waterwheels, too. They crushed rock to extract (remove) the metals.

From water mills to water turbines

The Industrial Revolution was the time when people first began using machines to make large amounts of goods. This period began in Britain in the 1700s. The Industrial Revolution spread from Britain to Europe and beyond. Hydropower was important in the early days of the Industrial Revolution. The first large factories were **water mills**. The water mills used hydropower to run the machines that made textiles (cloth).

Steam power soon replaced water mills in the Industrial Revolution. Hydropower did not disappear, however. During the 1800s, scientists developed new kinds of waterwheels, called water **turbines**. Waterwheels were large and turned slowly. Water turbines were smaller and turned at high speeds. Soon, water turbines were being used instead of waterwheels to power textile mills and sawmills.

Making electricity

In the late 1800s, people began using water turbines to produce electricity. Electricity made this way is called **hydroelectricity**.

The very first electric power plant was water-powered. It opened in Godalming, Britain, in 1881. A waterwheel in the river produced enough electricity for streetlights and lighting for a few buildings. The power plant soon closed because it was too expensive to run. Before long, many more powerful hydroelectric power plants appeared.

KEY WORDS

hydropower: power that comes from water's energy. (*Hydro* means "water.")
turbine: a type of engine powered by a flow of fluid. Turbines have large blades that spin, creating energy.
water mill: a mill (a factory with machines for processing materials) using machines that run on hydropower
waterwheel: a wheel turned by falling or running water

CHAPTER THREE

HYDROELECTRICITY

The use of hydroelectricity has grown fast since the 1800s. Today, hydroelectric power supplies about 20 percent of the world's electricity. In the United States, about 7 percent of the electricity comes from this source. Canada gets more than 70 percent of its electricity from hydroelectric power. Other countries get even more. Norway and Paraguay, for example, make nearly all their electricity from hydroelectric power.

How it works

Hydroelectric power plants need a source of flowing water. They are often built inside a **dam** that crosses a river. As the flow of river water backs up behind the dam, a **reservoir** forms. A reservoir is an artificial lake. People use reservoirs for recreational purposes, such as swimming, boating, and fishing. The reservoir may also provide water for farms, homes, and businesses. Reservoir water allows the hydroelectric plant to keep operating even if the flow of water in the river decreases.

Dams can be nearly any size. Those that contain power plants are usually massive structures, however. They must hold back millions of tons (tonnes) of water. Some are wide enough to allow a full-sized road to be built across the top.

HOOVER DAM

Dams are among the biggest structures built by humans. The Hoover Dam is on the Nevada-Arizona border near Las Vegas. It is 726 feet (221 meters) high. The dam was built across a deep canyon in the Colorado River between 1931 and 1936. The entire river was diverted through two huge tunnels while the dam was being built.

Hoover Dam — originally called the Boulder Canyon Dam — supplies power to roughly fourteen million people in the Southwest. A road runs across the top of the dam, which created Lake Mead.

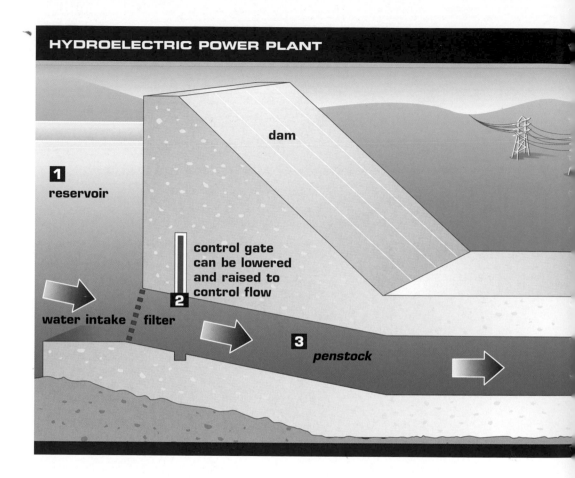

HYDROELECTRIC POWER PLANT

dam

1 reservoir

control gate
can be lowered
and raised to
control flow

2

water intake · filter

3 *penstock*

Most dams are built across the narrowest part of a river. A dam's design depends on its location. Some dams rely on their great size to hold back the water and form a reservoir. Others use a curved shape to block water. The reservoir forms in what was the natural river valley.

A dam may also be a combination of designs. No matter the shape of the dam, however, any hydroelectric power plant within it works basically the same way. **Gravity** makes water flow downhill. The flowing water is used to produce electricity.

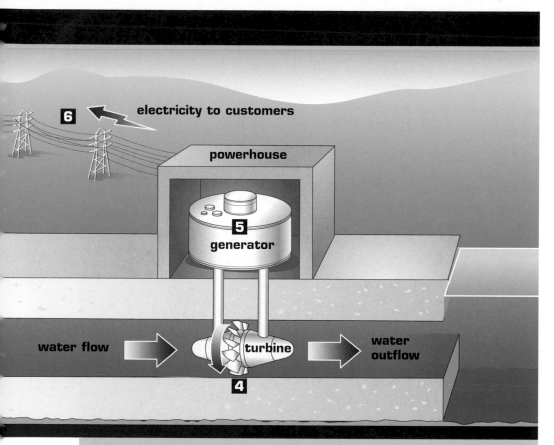

electricity to customers

6

powerhouse

5

generator

water flow

turbine

water outflow

4

The dam for a hydroelectric power plant holds back water to create a reservoir (1). A control gate controls the flow of water. When the gate is open (2), water flows along the **penstock** (3). The force of the water spins the blades of the water turbine (4). The spinning turbine turns the **generator** (5). This produces electricity. Overhead electric power lines (6) carry electricity from the power plant to homes and industries.

Making hydroelectricity

Some kinds of hydroelectric power plants can be used to store energy as well as make it. This energy supply is known as pumped storage. The demand for electricity is always changing. It can be high at one time and low at another. When demand is

FISH FRIENDLY

Dams stop fish and other water animals from moving freely up and down a river. Turbines can kill fish. Scientists at the U.S. Department of Energy are working on the design of a new, "fish-friendly" turbine. Fish can swim right through this turbine and survive the trip. Many dams also have fish ladders for fish that need to swim upstream. A fish ladder looks like steps that run alongside a dam. Fish, such as salmon, can jump from one level to the next highest to move upriver.

Fish, such as salmon, can travel upstream around a dam by using a fish ladder. The fish keep jumping up or swimming from one step of the fish ladder to the next highest to reach the other side of the dam without injury.

low, power plants have extra electricity. This electricity can be used to pump water uphill into a second, higher reservoir. When the demand for electricity is high, the water in the higher reservoir is released. It rushes down through a turbine that makes electricity.

TOP DAMS

Most power:	China's Three Gorges Dam will produce 18,200 **megawatts** of electric power when finished in 2009.
Tallest:	Rogun Dam in Tajikistan is 1,099 feet (335 meters) tall.
Most material:	Syncrude Tailings Dam in Alberta, Canada, contains more than 700 million cubic yards (540 million cubic meters) of earth and rock.
Biggest reservoir:	Lake Volta in Ghana, Africa, covers an area of nearly 3,300 square miles (8,500 square kilometers).

Good and bad

Hydroelectric power seems like an ideal way to generate electricity. Water in rivers and lakes is constantly replenished by rainfall. Hydroelectric power is also free of pollution. Water turbines do not produce any polluting gases.

Large dams and hydro-electric power plants have some problems, however. Building a large dam is a huge task that takes many years. The costs are enormous. Once the dam is built, a large area of land is flooded to make the reservoir. People and wildlife have to move out of

The ancient temple of Ramses II, with its four enormous seated statues carved into rock, was originally built near Abu Simbel, Egypt. That area was flooded by the construction of the Aswan High Dam. Completed in 1970, the dam created a reservoir called Lake Nasser. In an enormous engineering feat, the temple was cut up and relocated to higher ground.

the area. More than one million people have lost their homes to make space for the Three Gorges Dam on the Yangtze River in China.

Dams also make the water flow more slowly.

Silt and mud sinks to the riverbed. Silt can sometimes fill up a reservoir, making the power plant useless. The reduced flow can also affect water supplies for people downstream from the dam.

Low-head power

The **head** of a hydroelectric power plant is the distance the water drops as it flows through the plant. Power plants that produce a lot of electricity need a high head of water to work efficiently. Low-head power plants can still produce electricity, but not as much. They also do not need a large dam or reservoir to produce power.

Smaller power plants with low heads are built on smaller rivers. Such smaller hydropower plants do not cause a large reservoir to form. Instead, an underwater pipe upriver from the plant channels water into the turbine.

Most low-head power plants are considered micro (small) power plants. They produce only enough electricity to power a few homes. Micro-hydro systems can be built cheaply where other hydroelectric power may not work. Micro-hydropower is used in many countries. China, for example, has more than 85,000 micro-hydropower plants.

KEY WORDS

dam: a barrier to stop the flow of water

head: the distance water falls in a hydroelectric power plant

hydroelectricity: electricity made from water power

megawatt: a measurement of power produced. One megawatt is one million watts. A watt is the amount of electrical energy flowing in one second. Electrical energy is measured in units called joules. One watt is the same as one joule per second.

reservoir: a body of water that forms a lake behind a dam

CHAPTER FOUR

ENERGY IN THE OCEAN

Hydroelectric power is an important source of energy in many countries. There are other kinds of water power, however. These sources use the ocean's tides, waves, and stored energy. The energy in the ocean could supply power for the future.

Using the tides

Tides happen because of the regular rise and fall of sea levels. This change is caused mostly by the pull of the Moon's gravity acting on Earth. The Sun's gravity also pulls on the oceans somewhat.

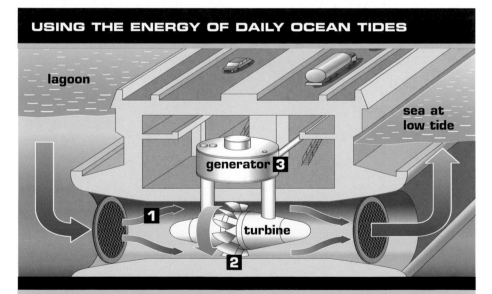

USING THE ENERGY OF DAILY OCEAN TIDES

lagoon

sea at low tide

generator **3**

1

turbine

2

At low tide, water in the **lagoon** is allowed to flow toward the sea through a turbine (1). As the water turns the turbine blades (2), the generator (3) makes electricity. At high tide, seawater flows back into the lagoon.

THE BIGGEST TIDES

The Bay of Fundy on the east coast of Canada has the world's largest tidal range. The water can rise and fall as much as 56 feet (17 meters). A location with such large tidal changes is a good place for a tidal power plant. A small tidal power plant has been built in the Bay of Fundy at Annapolis Royal. The location of that power plant has caused some erosion (wearing away) of the coast, however.

One way to use the power of the tides is to build a barrier across the mouth of a bay. The barrier has gates that open and close. It also contains turbines. As the tide comes in, ocean water flows into the bay through the turbines and generates electricity. The barrier's gates then close to keep the water inside the bay. When it is time for the tide to go out, the water flow reverses direction and pushes seaward against the barrier.

The gates then open, and water rushes out the opposite way, toward the sea. As water again flows through the turbines, more electricity is produced.

Certain areas on Earth have stronger tides than others. A tidal power plant needs a water level change of at least 16 feet (5 meters) between high and low tides. At present, there is only one large tidal power plant. It is at La Rance in France (*see page 24*). There are smaller plants in Canada, China, and Norway. New tidal power plants are being planned in many other countries, including Korea, Australia, Mexico, Russia, and the United States.

Tidal stream generators can also produce electricity from tidal flow. They use underwater propellers that get energy from the movement of water. Engineers must find ways to keep water plants and animals from being harmed by the propellers. Tidal stream generators are still very new, but they have great **potential**.

The La Rance River tidal power plant near Saint Malo, France, has been in operation for more than forty years. La Rance produces enough electricity to provide power to a large city.

Wave power

Another way to get energy from the ocean is to use the power of waves. Many people are experimenting with ways of using wave power. It is not as reliable as tidal power. So far, no major wave power plants have been built.

SALTER'S DUCK

In the 1970s, Professor Stephen Salter of Edinburgh University in Britain invented the "Salter's duck." Shaped like an aircraft wing, it made electricity from waves. The "duck" floated on the surface but was fastened to the seabed. It bobbed up and down on the waves. Its movements generated electricity.

Salter's design is still one of the most efficient wave-power devices ever invented. It can turn 90 percent of the energy of the waves into electricity. Salter's ducks are expensive to make, however. No power plant currently uses them.

Engineers have tried different ways of generating electricity from waves. One way uses a hollow, floating chamber that lets the waves flow in and out. When waves roll in, they push air up and out through an airshaft. The rushing air turns an air turbine (a kind of windmill). The turbine turns a generator that makes electricity. When the waves flow out of the chamber, air is drawn back through the turbine. This also produces electricity.

Other methods use devices that bob on the water's surface. They look like airplane wings, bobbing corks, or floating snakes. The "snakes" line up parallel with the waves and shoreline. The snakes are linked together by mooring lines that keep them straight. Snakes contain equipment that converts wave energy to electricity. The electricity travels to shore through cables.

Wave power plants must be located where there are large waves most of the time. They will need to operate in a wide range of weather conditions. Engineers hope to someday develop a good wave power system. Wave power plants could supply up to 5 percent of the world's energy. Like other kinds of hydropower, wave power is renewable and does not cause pollution.

Using ocean temperatures

The ocean collects huge amounts of energy each day.

Toronto, Canada, on Lake Ontario uses a system that cools office buildings near the waterfront. The system produces enough power to also cool nearly seven thousand homes in the surrounding area.

Even so, the Sun heats only the uppermost layer of the ocean. This means that the ocean is warm at the surface and cold deeper underwater. A process called **ocean thermal energy conversion** (OTEC) uses differences in water temperatures to create energy.

OTEC uses warm seawater from the surface and cold water from the ocean depths to power a turbine. The OTEC system uses several sets of pipes. One pipe contains the warm surface water. Another set holds liquid ammonia. **Heat exchangers** transfer the heat. Heat from the water pipes warms the pipes holding the ammonia. The liquid ammonia boils at a low temperature. It changes into a gas. The gas spins a turbine and generates electricity.

Next, another set of pipes comes into play. It holds cold water from the ocean depths. The cold water pipes cool down the pipes containing ammonia gas. The gas condenses into liquid ammonia, and the whole process starts over. OTEC is still an expensive way to produce electricity.

KEY WORDS

heat exhangers: a system consisting of sets of pipes that contain hot and cold liquids; the heat or cold transfers between the pipes to turn fluids to gases or gases to fluids

ocean thermal energy conversion: a process that uses the different levels of temperature in ocean water to make electricity

potential: future possibilities

tides: the regular rise and fall of ocean water levels that occurs twice daily

CHAPTER FIVE

WATER POWER FOR THE FUTURE

Today, water power is the most successful source of renewable energy. Making electricity from water is cheap and **efficient**. It also produces little pollution.

Small power plants and ocean energy

In the future, using more hydroelectric power will help reduce pollution and slow down global warming. There are limits to how many large hydroelectric plants we can build. But there are many places where micro-hydro systems can be used. They could supply a small area or even just one house. Micro-hydropower could greatly increase the amount of electricity we get from water.

People may someday get large amounts of energy from the oceans. Tidal stream generators and wave power could make large amounts of electricity. Floating OTEC power plants could produce a lot of energy, too.

There are still challenges facing the use of ocean energy. One of them is that saltwater causes **corrosion**. The salt slowly eats away at metal parts used in power plants. Scientists are constantly working on ways to solve these kinds of problems.

The energy problem

In the future, we will use several different forms of energy. Wind power and

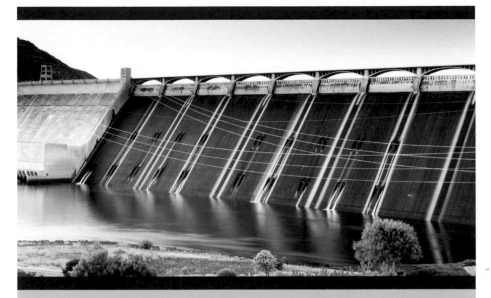

Grand Coulee Dam, on the Columbia River, in Washington state is the largest concrete structure in the United States. The power plant has four powerhouses that produce up to 6,500 megawatts of electricity. It is the largest producer of hydroelectric power in the United States.

solar energy (energy from sunlight) will be important. **Biofuels** — fuels made from plant and animal matter — will also be part of the mix. So will hydrogen gas. By itself, hydropower could never completely replace fossil fuels. But it will play an important part in supplying our future energy needs.

KEY WORDS

biofuels: fuels made from biomass (material from plants or animals). Wood is a biofuel. Corn oil, restaurant waste, or other natural plant products can be used as biofuel.

corrosion: act of eating away at something

efficient: working well and without much waste

GLOSSARY

dam: a barrier to stop the flow of water

developing nation: a country that is starting to build industries, or industrialize. These countries usually have fast-growing populations. Many developing nations stayed poor while other nations in North America and Western Europe grew rich.

efficient: working well and without much waste

emissions: substances let out into the air, such as carbon dioxide given off by burning coal or oil

fossil fuels: fuels formed in the ground over millions of years, including coal, oil, and natural gas

generator: a machine that uses fuel to make electrical energy

gravity: an attractive force that pulls objects together. Earth, the Moon, and the Sun all pull objects toward themselves because of the force of gravity.

hydroelectricity: electricity made from hydropower (water power). It is also called hydroelectric power.

hydropower: power that comes from water's energy. (Hydro means water.)

lagoon: an area of water separated from the sea by a barrier

penstock: channel or pipe along which water flows to a turbine

potential: future possibilities

power plant: a factory that produces electricity

reservoir: a lake that forms behind a dam

TOP EIGHT ENERGY SOURCES

in alphabetical order

The following list highlights the major fuel sources of the twenty-first century.
It also lists some advantages and disadvantages of each:

	Advantages	Disadvantages
Biofuels	renewable energy source; widely available from a number of sources, including farms, restaurants, and everday garbage	fossil fuels often used to grow farm crops; requires special processing facilities that run on fossil fuels in order to produce usable biofuel
Fossil fuels: coal, oil, petroleum	used by functioning power plants worldwide; supports economies	limited supplies; emit greenhouse gases; produce toxic wastes; must often be transported long distances
Geothermal energy	nonpolluting; renewable; free source	available in localized areas; would require redesign of heating systems
Hydrogen (fuel cells)	most abundant element in the universe; nonpolluting	production uses up fossil fuels; storage presents safety issues
Nuclear energy	produces no greenhouse gases; produces a lot of energy from small amounts of fuel	solid wastes remain dangerous for centuries; limited life span of power plants
Solar power	renewable; produces no pollutants; free source	weather and climate dependent; solar cells expensive to manufacture
Water power	renewable resource; generally requires no additional fuel	requires flowing water, waves, or tides; can interfere with view; dams may destroy large natural areas and disrupt human settlements
Wind power	renewable; nonpolluting; free source	depends on weather patterns; depends on location; endangers bird populations

RESOURCES

Books

Parker, Steve. *Water Power.*
Science Files: Energy (series).
Gareth Stevens (2004)

Petersen, Christine.
Alternative Energy.
True Books (series).
Children's Press (2004)

Web Sites

www.pbs.org/tesla/ins/niagara.html
View an animated diagram that shows how the Niagara River is used to make electricity.

www.eia.doe.gov/kids/energyfacts/ sources/renewable/ocean.html
Learn more about water power from the U.S. Department of Energy Web site that explores ocean energy.

Publisher's note to educators and parents: Our editors have carefully reviewed these Web sites to ensure that they are suitable for children. Many Web sites change frequently, however, and we cannot guarantee that a site's future contents will continue to meet our high standards of quality and educational value. Be advised that children should be closely supervised whenever they access the Internet.

INDEX

MELCHER ON ACQUISITION

Daniel Melcher

with

Margaret Saul

 American Library Association

Chicago 1971

International Standard Book Number 0-8389-0108-5 (1971)

Library of Congress Catalog Card Number 77-158719

Printed in the United States of America

Contents

Preface

This book originally set out to be a kind of reporting-in-depth of the American Library Association Pre-Conference on Acquisitions held in Atlantic City in the summer of 1969—a report embracing not only the essential content of the formal speeches, but also the floor discussions and after-hours bull sessions.

Meanwhile, however, a closely similar treatment of the problem of how to buy library materials, long in process, suddenly shaped up and was published by ALA in November 1969. This was *Purchasing Library Materials in Public and School Libraries* by Evelyn Hensel and Peter D. Veillette.

A treatment of the acquisition process in college and university libraries was also taking shape at this time and became the January 1970 issue of *Library Trends*. The acquisition problems of research libraries were likewise getting detailed examination in the two annual International Seminars on Approval and Gathering Plans in Large and Medium Size Academic Libraries, sponsored by Western Michigan University in the fall of 1968 and the fall of 1969. Peter Spyers-Duran prepared published reports of these seminars: *Approval and Gathering Plans in Academic Libraries* (Peter Spyers-Duran, ed., Libraries Unlimited, Inc., Littleton, Colo., 1969) and *Advances in Understanding Approval and Gathering Plans in Academic Libraries* (Peter Spyers-Duran, ed., Western Michigan University Press, Kalamazoo, 1970).

What with the coverage of school and public libraries in the Hensel and Veillette report (in which the appendixes covering form letters, questionnaires, book bids, and contracts are especially valuable) and the coverage of research library problems in *Library Trends* and the Spyers-Duran efforts, it began to seem redundant to go ahead with a straightforward report of a conference at which so many of the very same views had been presented. I therefore decided to take a fresh look at my assignment and set out to reorient it to take best advantage of what I had to bring to the problem, namely, the publisher's viewpoint.

What follows is, therefore, a personal set of observations on the acquisitions process, to which I bring twenty-one years of experience with the R. R. Bowker Co. (where I initiated *Books in Print, Subject Guide, American Book Publishing Record, Forthcoming Books*, etc.), and to which Margaret Saul (Mrs. Melcher) brings seven years of experience as the editor of the *School Library Journal* and further experience as a consultant to publishers on reaching the library market.

Our special thanks are due to Ann Heidbreder, whose constant encouragement kept us at work, and to Dorothy Deininger and Harold Roth, who gave freely of their time and advice.

DANIEL MELCHER

MELCHER ON ACQUISITION

Goals in Library Acquisition

Fundamentally, the wants of any library's users are easily stated. They want what they want—now.

They want it when it is being reviewed, talked about, displayed in bookstore windows, or offered in coupon ads. If you haven't got it yet, but it is in the bookstore across the street, they don't see *why* you haven't got it. If it's in the library but not yet cataloged, they don't see why that should prevent you from letting them take it out. If last year's issues of X magazine have been reported in the bindery for the past six months, they don't see why you send the issues to the bindery before the bindery is ready to bind them.

It should scarcely be necessary to rehearse the wants of a library's patrons—they re-present themselves every day—and besides, we have all been borrowers. It is astonishing, though, how quickly and easily the convenience of the public can be subordinated to the convenience of the staff, unless some staff member with influence in high places and the courage to use it can appoint himself ombudsman and constantly question unthinking disservices to the readers.

I don't know how long the magazines at the New York Public Library spend in the bindery, but I get the feeling that they vanish from public access the instant the librarian can assemble an unbroken run for binding, regardless of when the bindery can get at them. I know why this is done, but I don't like it.

The libraries of the New York City public schools were for years required to select books from a list which was itself about a year in the making, and the books had to be ordered by a process which ensured that they would not be received for about another year. In company with other concerned publishers and citizens I met several times with officials of the school system, and we were assured at every meeting that action was being taken, but the years went by and so far as I know (up to the present writing) it is not even claimed that more than a fraction of the school librarians have had any relief on more than a fraction of their purchases. Of course, the current drive for drastic decentralization of the whole New York City school system has the decentralization of book selection and book ordering as one of its objectives.

If some of your library's time-hallowed procedures seem to come between your patrons and the services they seek, you may find some answers in the chapters which follow. At least you'll find how others have solved their problems, and you may get ideas for solving yours.

You'll notice one thing, though. No one has come up with any all-purpose magic formula. Problem solving still begins at home, and it begins with a careful review of your goals. Prepackaged solutions aren't available as yet and probably aren't near enough to be worth waiting for.

What exactly do your library users want from you? Is there any reason why you can't set yourself the goal of giving them exactly what they want? What stands between you and such a goal?

The lovely thing about such goal analysis is that on the first round you needn't and you shouldn't do anything less than dream big. Remember the admonition, "Dream no small dreams; they have no power to stir men's minds." Remember also the rule that "a problem well stated is half solved."

First and foremost, however, the dreams need to be dreamed in terms of what the users want. Ask of every new proposal, such as a move to automation or central processing or centralized receiving, in what way this will make for better service to the user. Keeping the user constantly in mind is almost your only defense against sliding into procedures that perhaps make things easier for one clerk, but make things harder for your entire public. Eternal vigilance is the price of freedom from thoughtlessly burdensome procedures.

Solutions that have grass roots, i.e., solutions that grow out of the problem, are always to be preferred to prepackaged solutions imported from elsewhere. The latter are usually about as satisfactory as mail-order dentures.

2

There are a lot of figures in this book. Skip them if you don't find them interesting, but I hope you will give them at least a bit of atten- tion. The more you know about the economics of those you buy from, the more effectively you can deal with them. One of the basic goals of this book is to explain why things are as they are; and to understand why a situation is as it is often requires a look at the economics of the situation. There is a reason for everything. This book aims to throw light on the reasons for some of our existing problems and it hopes to suggest solutions to them.

Although some book acquisition problems originate outside the library and are beyond the control of any one library, a good many problems are really of internal origin and fully susceptible to solution through internal action. Diligent pursuit of the following objectives would help (these are all dealt with at greater length in later chapters):

Find a way to buy service instead of discount. The great majority of libraries of all types have long since won their freedom from blind acceptance of the low bid. You can, too. You must.

Encumber only upon receipt. If necessary, have an agreement in writing with the supplier that all his shipments are "on approval" until paid for, though you do not expect to take advantage of this.

Pay on the supplier's invoice; ask no special billing.

Pay promptly. Pay for partial shipments. Pay invoices as rendered; spot-check their accuracy later. If you are dealing with a reputable supplier, you can be sure he won't hesitate to rectify errors found later.

Order often. Don't keep your readers waiting. An order of 50 to 100 books is not too small.

Simplify your paper work. Make one writing meet all needs. Order by slip, not list. Have no more than five parts to your form set.

Get what you order. Enforce your contracts. Spot-check performance.

Know your inside costs. Let your supplier do anything he can do cheaper.

How Long Should It Take to Get a Book?

Any library which orders only twice a year (as many schools do) is plainly saying, "Time doesn't matter to us." This may not be the way the librarian feels. He may wish desperately that he could have a needed book sent over at once from the nearest bookstore, a privilege many an individual book buyer takes for granted. He may count himself the prisoner of a system set up for the procurement of more predictable things like pencils or school buses. He may feel helpless to break out of the system.

Let him take heart from the knowledge that more and more schools *are* persuading the system that any library which cannot provide this month's book this month is a backward library. What reader, teacher, or student wants to be limited in his reading to the books everyone else stopped talking about a year ago?

One major jobber comments:

> We wish all libraries would order frequently rather than once or twice a year. They'd not only get their books faster; they'd have a better chance of getting the books at all—before they go out of print. And we could be more efficient at our end if we didn't have these peak loads.
>
> Our bookstore customers order daily—and expect us to ship within 24 hours. We give their orders a priority because it is so clear that they *care*. Their customers are waiting.
>
> Some public libraries, too, seem to be conscious of the fact that their customers are waiting, and if their pattern of

ordering shows it, we try to cooperate to the limit. Shipment of books from stock within a routine 48 hours of receipt of order isn't too much to ask for.

But you can bet that our people don't give much of a priority to school orders that the customer himself has been sitting on for up to six months.

Six months? Some libraries order only once a year, apparently because this is a pattern that seems to work in such areas as school supplies, textbooks, laboratory equipment, and so forth.

How long *should* it take a library to get a book? In terms of goals, why let your library settle for less than the best? If other libraries are getting two-day or seven-day service and you are getting two-month or one-year service, don't take it lying down. Make waves.

In the greater New York and Los Angeles areas, bookstores can typically say, "Sorry, we seem to be out of that, but I think we could have it for you tomorrow." They can say this because they routinely phone in their replacement needs to their wholesaler each day and get delivery on the next truck. The same wholesalers are quite happy to extend the same service to libraries, provided the libraries don't burden the relationship with excessive red tape.

Whether or not overnight service might be available in your area, one-week service is a goal within the reach of almost everyone, and two-week service ought to be considered the outer limit. Many a public library, for example, routinely sends off a weekly order and routinely expects the resulting shipment within a week or so. After all, no more than 24 hours should elapse between posting of the order and its receipt by the wholesaler. If the wholesaler thinks you care, he can certainly ship what's in stock within 48 hours, if not 24. The mails may be slow, but still four days should and usually do suffice to see the books from wholesaler to library.

All this may seem like belaboring the obvious to any library which routinely expects and gets such service. There are, however, an astonishing number of libraries in which such service is unknown and such a goal would sound utopian. In too many elementary school libraries it has long been routine to order annually in the spring and then wait six months or more for receipt of any of the books.

The order librarian in a large eastern university writes: "Perhaps the loudest 'beef' of the faculty is that the local bookstores and the University Store will have books on display which have not yet been received on standing order here at the library. Unfortunately, the University Store limits the amount we can purchase from them."

It is never possible, of course, to count on your wholesaler having everything you want in stock. Apart from out-of-print material, some

5

of the titles you order may be NYP (not yet published). Some may be TOS (temporarily out of stock), which ought to mean that the wholesaler will get some soon. Some may be "out of stock/no date," which can mean anything.

If you want a book your wholesaler doesn't handle, how long does it take to get it direct from the publisher? This varies enormously, of course. Some publishers routinely ship within 48 hours. Some (the more automated ones) expect to ship about the fifth day after receipt of order. Any of them will, of course, be slower if it is their policy to put large orders ahead of small, or if the book is out of stock but expected, or if peak demands have put them behind, or if they are going through a period of chaos resulting from badly planned automation.

There isn't much you can do about this kind of delay, but there is another kind over which you can exercise some control; namely, the delay that results when the publisher's order clerk takes one look at your order and moves it quickly from the top of the pile to the bottom, thinking, "Better I spend the next hour filling a dozen no-problem orders than spend it struggling through the fine print on this one." (More about this in a later chapter, "Toward Tighter Goals and Norms in Book Ordering Procedures.")

How long *should* it take to get a book direct from the publisher? The answer that is given year after year at the annual convention of the American Booksellers Association is, "A lot less time than it *does* take."

By the standards of many other industries (prescription drugs, for one), book distribution is needlessly inefficient from top to bottom. It is high time the publishers' customers spoke up and demanded something better. As things now stand, the priorities are all wrong. Everybody is trying to save pennies instead of days, even though the saving of a penny at the cost of a day is a pretty poor exchange.

I know because it happened to me. When I was head of Bowker, I used to be told that orders received today were shipped tomorrow. Only they weren't. This was what employees told the boss, because it was what he wanted to hear, but it wasn't what happened. In the early spring the big January orders put us "temporarily" behind. In April the advance work on the *Trade List Annual* put us "temporarily" behind. In the summer it was vacations that put us "temporarily" behind. In the fall the handling of the big *Books in Print* orders put us "temporarily" behind.

It was "policy" that the shipping room should work overtime as necessary to keep up with the orders. But, as a practical matter, the head of the shipping room found it more expedient to please the treasurer by keeping down the overtime than to please the customers by keeping up with the orders.

In terms of long-range goals, what can librarians and booksellers do to bring pressure on the publishers to stop kidding themselves about their fulfillment performance and really devise staff incentives that get results?

One step in the right direction would be to monitor performance and really let top management know how things are. In England annual publicity is given to the publishers who do the best fulfillment job. In America there has been only one such survey, to my knowledge. However, even if publishers agreed to give priority handling to orders written on some kind of standard (simplified) order form, could your library take advantage of it?

It may be argued that there is another approach to the problem of the patron who wants a book the library doesn't own, namely, interlibrary loan. This often helps, but all too often a book suddenly in demand in your library is suddenly in demand elsewhere, too.

Should a library stand ready to buy any book that a patron requests, even if the book was previously passed over during the regular selection procedure? Well, some libraries do it routinely and report that the payoff in good public relations is enormous in proportion to the comparatively small cost. Such a policy doesn't open the floodgates, and it can provide the kind of feedback from the readers that a good selection staff welcomes.

(Not all book selectors are so humble, of course. I once asked a very well-known public librarian how she identified her selection mistakes. She was indignant. "We don't make selection mistakes," she said icily. I said: "Oh, go on, everybody does. Even the best booksellers find themselves returning up to 25 percent of the books they buy. Surely there are books on your shelves that you thought would be in demand but which, in fact, have never been opened. I bet your book selectors would like to know which they are." She said, "There may be books on our shelves that have never been opened, but that's not *our* mistake, that's our readers' mistake.")

Some means of getting books fast can also be important when the library owns a title, perhaps in multiple copies, but none of the copies is ever on the shelf. When this situation is discovered, a good case can be made for reduplication of the title. All of us old enough to remember the Great Depression cannot help shuddering a little at the idea of rushing out to buy a title the library already owns, merely because it is not on the shelf when sought. Yet there is hardly any kind of book expenditure more certain to produce a tangible payout in reader

7

satisfaction than one aimed straight at serving a reader hanging over your desk and panting for the book *now*.

In passing, I remember a story Eric Moon told me about trying to keep a copy of *War and Peace* on the shelf in the public library of Westminster, London. He made a list of this and 25 other classics which the library owned (of course) but which were just never in. He decided to duplicate, and reduplicate, and re-reduplicate these ever-popular classics until a browser would have a fighting chance of seeing one on the shelves once in a while. As I recall, it took about 25 copies of *War and Peace* to achieve that goal.

One might ask: What has this to do with the value of time? Surely the duplication of a classic need not be done in haste. But from the reader's viewpoint, what good is a library that is full of books but empty of any that interest him?

To recap: A library needs a *method* of getting a book *fast*. The bulk of its book buying can perhaps be handled more deliberately, but there are very few situations where a library can reasonably buy as if it were buying solely for posterity.

Obviously it makes little difference whether a book that won't be published until two months hence is ordered this week or next. The need for replacements can sometimes be anticipated. Seasonal demands can be anticipated. Not every book is needed or wanted within a few days of the decision to buy it. On the other hand, what library does not need at least a *procedure* for the "rush" procurement of books, the need for which was not anticipated?

Of course, there can be a price on speed. When a book can be had from a wholesaler at 36 percent off list and from a nearby retailer at only 20 percent off list, the difference may be 16 percent off list—or, on a $6 book, about $1. However, many a library would spend as much or more just on the paper work incident to cumulating and processing an order for the same book placed through normal channels.

From another point of view, it is not abnormal to devote an hour of staff time—an hour that may cost the taxpayer a good $10 in salary, fringe benefits, and related overheads—to the satisfying of a single inquiry. In this context it could hardly be termed extravagant to spend just $1 to satisfy another type of inquiry through an authorization to pick up a needed volume at Blank's Bookstore.

How Important Is Promptness in the Acquisitions Process?

Time is a purchasable commodity. You can order in the usual way and wait the usual time and get the usual discount. Or, at the other extreme, you can pay for long-distance phone calls, messengers, taxis, or whatever it takes to save time, in which situation the matter of what discount you get will seem entirely irrelevant.

E. B. Jackson of IBM tells of the time a General Motors assembly line broke down in Pontiac, Michigan. The line stayed down until a book on how to get it going again came in from Detroit under police escort, screaming sirens and all.

Another IBM librarian told me once how he had a U.S. book flown in from Paris. He hadn't been able to locate a copy anywhere in New York. The publisher was out of stock. He knew, though, that the IBM branch managers would jump through hoops for anything wanted by IBM world headquarters. In response to his transatlantic phone call, IBM/Paris located a copy in Brentano's/Paris and had it on a New York flight within a couple of hours.

Not all books are needed so urgently. On the other hand, the time when a book is most likely to be most useful is the period immediately following the decision to buy it.

I have seen some blatant examples of situations in which time values seem to have been ignored. Take *Books in Print*, for example. During my time at Bowker this regularly went to the printer the day after Labor Day, started through the bindery a week or so later, and the customer could expect his advance order to be filled during October. However, literally thousands of libraries would not even order until December, January, February, or March. Some may have decided late, of course, but others regularly, year after year, seemed to throw away, for no apparent reason, several months' use of what was, after all, a book with only a limited useful life.

In the case of an annual reference book that will have little or no reference value once its successor becomes available, the value of time is surely at least 8 percent a month. If a reference annual is worth $24 when it comes out and zero dollars 12 months later, it is clearly losing value at the rate of $2 a month, or about 8 percent a month, or 2 percent a *week*. If you ordered the annual from some discounter in Outer Mongolia to save 3 percent and had to wait an extra month as a result, you would clearly be out 5 percent, which would be a bad trade.

Not all books have such a predictable useful life, but there can't be many on which the loss of a month's use isn't a calculable loss. Take, for example, a current best seller. How much is the first month worth as against the second, third, or fourth? I think it can be assumed, from publishers' sales if nothing else, that the value of a book begins high and runs downhill. In many cases you will probably agree that the first month of a hot book's life is worth as much as 25 percent of the price. Then the value gradually drops.

Or take a perennial—*Robinson Crusoe*. What's the value of time if you are buying a replacement copy of *Robinson Crusoe*? You might say, "Well, time isn't worth anything, because we still have the old copy." If, however, you did not order the replacement until the old copy had broken in half, then the cost of not having *Robinson Crusoe* is surely something. I don't know what it is but let's say such a classic has a three-year life, so that the decision to own it is a decision that possession is worth at least 3 percent of its cost each month. This being the case, it is surely fair to suggest that the cost of not having the book measurably lowers your intended standards of service by a like amount.

As a rule of thumb, I would propose that time is worth about 1 percent a week, and that anybody who goes for that last percent of discount and thereby loses a week is making a bad trade.

This is not to say that time need *always* cost money. By and large, the bookstores which order daily and the public libraries which order weekly pay no more than the school system which orders annually. There isn't much difference between the cost of filling one $1,000 order and the cost of filling five $200 orders, and there is little or no difference between the cost of filling one $5,000 order and the cost of filling five $1,000 orders. (Of course, this would not be true of a wholesaler who carried no stock and had to accumulate a substantial backlog of orders before he could order in quantities large enough to command the best publisher discounts.)

Much more often you can measure the advantages of time saved in solid dollars and cents and have those advantages without so much as a penny of extra outlay, provided only that you gear all systems to eliminate needless delays.

All of us get our first lessons in economics in the home. There we grow up feeling that money is money, but time is only time. We tend to put no cash value on time—until we become an employer. Even then, many an employer groans when he adds a salary, but then proceeds to treat the time of the latest employee *as if* it cost nothing. He may unwittingly slip into procedures in which he feels justified in using $5 worth of staff time to save $2 worth of cash outlay merely because the $5 is already committed and the $2 isn't.

It must also be said that in many a salaried situation *most* of the personnel have a natural bias in *favor* of more salaries as against more outside expenditure. Since it isn't their money, they see nothing but advantage in any shift from outside to inside expenditure. Unhappily many a department head also suspects that, in the last analysis, his own salary prospects may be related more closely to the amount his department costs the library than to the amount it saves the library.

Top management, though, must concern itself with maximizing the reader service that can be wrung out of each budget dollar in any way possible. Happily, good reader service often costs less than poor reader service! If the overall cost in salaries and other relevant overheads of ordering, receiving, and paying for a book has been averaging $2 a book and the overall time has been averaging two months, then it is both possible and likely that a hard-nosed systems analysis aimed at cutting that two months to two weeks may *also* cut that $2 to $1.

To the extent that you spend more time and money on paper shuffling, you will have less to spend on service and books. And if your acquisition procedures are any more complex than those of a good bookstore, the result is both higher cost and lower service.

Speeding up the acquisition process is thus directly related to cutting down on paper work, and both pretty well require that the head man overcome his preference for delegating systems work and give his own systems some very close attention. In this area, expertise is far less important than motivation. Anyone can proliferate paper work, but cutting it back takes someone with perspective, authority, and tact.

Systems analysis can be rather fun, especially if you enjoy problem solving, because a real breakthrough can provide a lovely sense of accomplishment. I remember once the treasurer at Bowker suggested we go from a five-part bill to a six-part bill. His logic was persuasive, but very opportunely we received a survey of how other publishers did it, from which we both got the same message loud and clear: namely, that if you're using more than five copies, you are using too many. Some publishers were getting by with four parts. The survey explained how some publishers were using up to 13 parts, but it also showed that this not only cost more, but that the more copies used the less speed resulted.

So we didn't go to six parts. In fact, we took a harder look at the fifth part. We didn't get rid of it, but we did something almost as good. We stopped filing it. This is a case where sometimes perfectly delightful economies can come up in very simple ways. The fifth part was the copy that was kept until you paid and was then put in a "paid bill" file. What would you do with a piece of paper marked "paid" except file it? But the question, once raised, became very interesting. Why were we filing it? We weren't going to dun you for an amount you had already paid. And in a pinch we had the same information on another copy used for sales analysis.

The upshot was that we stopped filing paid bills and eventually stopped keeping them. We found that filing this particular form had been costing us about $10,000 a year in salaries and overhead, or about 10 cents per item filed. Ten cents at first seemed to me a lot for just filing one piece of paper once, but I have since come to believe that for a file of any size the cost is rarely less, and sometimes more.

This means that in forms design it hardly matters what you pay the printer; what counts is the 10 cents it will cost you to file each part. This isn't all labor, of course. Part of it is the cost of lighting, heating or cooling, and cleaning the space required; part is allowance for coffee breaks, vacation pay, sick leave, pension plans, and social security; and part is for supervision.

I used to think that the big thing in forms design was to make a single typing of the information serve every subsequent need—the so-called "one-writing" principle. An extra carbon was something you got for the cost of the paper, a penny or so. You may be able to buy a five-part form for under 5 cents, but it will cost you 50 cents before everybody concerned has filed all the parts, and it may cost double or triple that if the various filed parts are much consulted.

It could be argued that you file only some of the parts, the rest being sent elsewhere, but this is cold comfort when you realize that most of the parts will at least be filed within your own system, and the ones sent outside often generate yet more paper that has to be put in or checked with your inside files when it comes back. (It costs as much or more to take information *from* a file as it does to put information *into* a file.)

Some libraries use a three-part order slip: one for the dealer, one for the catalog cards, and one for the library. Some libraries use a six-part order slip: two for the dealer, one for the catalog cards, and three for the library. Some libraries use a multipart requisition slip. *And* some libraries use a six-part order slip: two for the business department, one for the catalog cards, and three for the library. The business department in turn creates a 10-part purchase order: three for the dealer (one of which must be returned with the shipment), two for the library, two for the general accounting office, one for the receiving department, and two for the business office. It can be said in defense of this latter monstrosity that it *usually* covers more than a single title, but sometimes it is used even when only a single book is to be ordered.

What if . . . what *if* federal book funds came with the stipulation that a library — to qualify for the funds — must prove it had streamlined its acquisition procedures to the point where no order involved more paper than a single five-part 3 x 5 order set? Could you qualify? If not, I bet you'd find a way to qualify, and you would make your money go farther in the process.

I have talked about paper work as if I enjoyed it. I do in a way. I don't think of it as grubby detail. I see it more as *liberation from drudgery*. Checking paper-work proliferation does pay off. It gets you wanted books sooner. It leaves you more money for books, insofar as you spend less for the paper work, and it gives your staff more time for creativity.

The Cost of Placing an Order

In many libraries the cost of placing even a single order for a single book can be $15 or more. In bookstores any such costly procedure would be unthinkable.

In libraries, the process may start with "making out a requisition." This is then converted into a purchase order, one copy of which goes to the department initiating the requisition, one to the vendor, one to the office which will eventually have to approve and pay the bill, one to the pending order file, one to "receiving," and so on. In bookstores they often make just an original for the vendor and a copy for themselves. In fact, sometimes the vendor gets *no* copy—just a phone call.

Some libraries have learned to handle small orders as efficiently as bookstores. How they do it is well worth study because there is a lot of money at stake, money that could far better go for books than for paper shuffling.

Most people are very much surprised the first time they calculate what it costs them to place an order. In fact, they are so startled their first reaction is to disbelieve, reject, or suppress the evidence. That's perhaps the major reason why we have so few usable figures on the subject. Depend on it, though: Unless you are very atypical, the cost to you of placing an order is higher than you think and probably higher than you need.

Complex procurement policies are sometimes defended on the ground that extra care is warranted because "we are spending public money." It should be noted, though, that the bookseller's interest in safety is no less keen; after all, he is spending *his own* money. He must pare his expenses to the bone because his costs must be less than his discounts; yet his systems must still work, otherwise a dishonest employee or supplier could rob him blind.

Estimating very roughly, a bookstore has about a $3 discount on an $8 book, a $1 discount on a $2.50 paperback, and a 40-cent discount on a 95-cent paperback. Considering that this must cover book postage, rent, utilities, advertising, clerk hire, taxes, etc., not much can be allowed for "acquisition." Again estimating very roughly, a library wholesaler works on about half the above margins. Here, too, not much can be allowed for "acquisition."

Costly procurement policies are sometimes also accepted on the basis of "What can you do? It's the law." Happily there is usually no law, state or local; there are merely administrative regulations, hallowed by time perhaps, but fully open to modification upon administrative review. Even where embodied in law, procedures are, of course, open to amendment and sometimes to discretionary administrative interpretation.

A useful exercise is to see how far you can go in matching the efficiency of your supplier in the handling of book orders. Take, for example, the distribution problem posed by the emergence of the higher-priced paperbacks, sometimes called "class" paperbacks to distinguish them from the "mass"-marketed (newsstand) kind and sometimes (rather invidiously) called "quality" paperbacks. These paperbacks did not flow readily through the mass-market newsstand channels. Neither were they made very welcome by the old-line library wholesalers, who naturally preferred handling $4 units containing an 80-cent markup to handling (say) $2 units containing a 40-cent markup.

Two suppliers tackled this problem head on, however, namely, A & A Distributors and NACSCORP (National Association of College Stores), both finding that their effective operating margins were in the neighborhood of 20 to 30 cents a volume, and both finding ways to make this suffice.

It was no coincidence that the wholesalers who solved the problem of handling class paperbacks on the available margins were looking first and foremost at the problem of supplying them to retailers. NACSCORP was serving only members of the National Association of College Stores. A & A had been serving primarily bookstores and made sharp distinctions between high-volume, low-paper-work customers like the bookstores and the more commonly low-volume or high-paper-work customers like schools and libraries.

15

Take the case of a paperback retailing at $2 and available to the wholesaler at perhaps $1 or so, and to the retailer at $1.20. Out of the 20 cents, the wholesaler must cover all of his salaries, rent, postage, and other overheads, interest on borrowed money, taxes, and so forth.

To be sure, paperbacks do usually move in larger quantities of a title than hardbounds. If a bookseller typically buys twos, threes, or fives when a library might be buying ones, that alone lowers unit costs.

But a library could do worse than set itself the goal of handling its end of its acquisition operations at least as economically as its own suppliers handle their end. It is fairly easy to make a current calculation of the operating margins your supplier probably has on the books you buy from him. You won't know accurately what discounts he gets from the publishers on hardbounds, but you might not go far astray if you put it at 46 percent.

Suppose, then, you bought 16,000 books from him last year having combined list prices of $100,000, and you paid him $64,000, and he paid the publishers $56,000 (to include postage). His gross operating margin on his business with you was, then, about $8,000 on the 16,000 volumes, or about 50 cents a volume. Out of this he had to take the cost of *his* acquisition procedures, shelving, storing, picking, packing, shipping, rent, taxes, and other overheads, including the cost of complying with your acquisition procedures.

A question for you to ask yourself is: Did you do as well? Start with that $8,000 which had to cover his end of the operation. Deduct what he must have spent in postage to get the books to you (unless postage was added to your bill). Would the remainder have sufficed to cover all your expenses in requisitioning, encumbering, ordering, receiving, checking, passing for payment, and paying, including a reasonable approximation of applicable salaries and fringe benefits, supervision, supplies, rent, and so forth, not only within the library but wherever else the process might have taken salaried time?

To take another approach, consider what it does cost, could cost, and should cost to acquire a single book, involving a separate order to a separate source of supply.

When I was at Bowker, many of the orders were for single copies, e.g., one *Literary Market Place,* to be shipped and billed. My best estimate of the cost of handling such an order was $1.50, which had to cover typing up a multipart invoice form, picking and shipping the book, filing one part under "accounts receivable," awaiting payment, receiving and depositing the payment, and removing the item from the "accounts receivable" file. The $1.50 "transaction cost" was an average. It certainly cost somewhat less when there were no complications, and somewhat more when the billing had to be done on special forms or in special ways.

Costs may have risen somewhat since I made the above estimates, but I have fairly firm, fairly recent estimates from another publisher, also heavily involved in many orders involving only a single copy, and he estimates his fulfillment costs at about $2.50 per transaction. I would attribute part of the difference to inflation, part to the fact that he is more automated than Bowker was at the time of the $1.50 calculation. (I never met any publisher who felt that automation had actually reduced his costs, whatever his hopes might have been. The British firm of Allen & Unwin, probably the most efficient publisher in the business, is still unautomated.)

Perhaps a practical question for any library to ask itself might be: "Do our acquisition costs average under $2 per order plus 50 cents per volume? If not, shouldn't we give a high priority to getting them down to this level, if not below it?"

It should be noted that you can't really give yourself an "E" for "Efficiency" if your in-library costs are reasonable but you don't know what they spend over in the city procurement office. It's the sum of all relevant costs that should be under study.

Furthermore, it shouldn't be hard to make some shrewd estimates even of costs which are outside your sphere of operations. Simply estimate what it would cost you to do what they do if you did it the way they do it. And by now, presumably, you have a good tally on your own overall costs and can readily estimate what each element in your paper work must cost if total paper work, multiplied by unit costs, is to equal total overall costs.

A really hard-nosed cost study often turns up fairly shocking facts. You might well find that your real cost of placing a single order for a single item is in excess of $10, or four times the $2.50 I was setting up as a reasonably attainable goal. If you find your single-copy cost is high, you *could* say to yourself, "Well, most of our business is with wholesalers, and a $10 cost just to go through the requisition-order-payment routine isn't too bad if there are 50 books on the order. Our average may not be too bad."

I would urge you, nevertheless, to develop a lower-cost way of placing your single-copy orders. You cannot avoid doing a certain amount of acquisition work in this way. You might as well do it economically. Even if you were to place only 500 single-copy orders a year, in the context of overall acquisitions of 16,000 volumes, there would still be a worthwhile saving to be made if you could pare the cost of those single-copy orders from (say) $10 to $2.50.

17

The great thing about paring transaction costs is of course the tangible inside saving. Less obvious, but also important in the long run, are the savings to your supplier. Generally speaking, the less paper work for you, the less for him.

I used to feel that Bowker's $1.50 transaction cost was a composite. It could have been $1 if all libraries had bought as simply as did bookstores. The only reason it got to be $1.50 was because some libraries had procedures that ran the costs closer to $3. In fact, I once estimated that filling an order from the New York City schools cost close to $9, even for a single copy of a single paperback to a single address. As a general rule, I would estimate that at that time the list price of every Bowker book could have been knocked down by 50 cents if *all* libraries had been using as simple a method of ordering as some did.

Our transaction costs didn't seem trivial, so I did something that made me extraordinarily unpopular. I put on a $1 service charge for excessive processing, meaning that if we were required to bill on the customer's forms, have them notarized, signed by the treasurer, and so on, there would have to be a $1 charge. We didn't really want the dollar. But it did seem that the many should not have to pay for the red tape of the few. Some of the few paid the dollar without complaint. Others were furious, apparently convinced that their expansive forms had been ordained by God and were immutable, and that we were flying in the face of Providence even to cavil about them.

I hired a young law student named Nancy Paige to investigate the legal necessity for complex buying procedures. She went at it state by state and demonstrated, as we had suspected, that there are very few places where much of the red tape is really a matter of law at all. I don't think we found more than three states where there seemed to be any rule that couldn't have been overturned at the local level. In California there seemed, at first, to be a law, but closer study revealed that it had been amended in its application to books. In New Jersey some libraries swore that the red tape was beyond their control; others seemed to have no trouble avoiding it. I think I recall putting some of the former libraries in touch with some of the latter. Since that date the state of New Jersey has adopted a law exempting all public libraries from bid requirements:

SENATE, NO. 480

STATE OF NEW JERSEY

INTRODUCED FEBRUARY 13, 1968

By Senator HIERING

Referred to Committee on County and Municipal Government

An Act concerning purchases of library materials by free public libraries and supplementing chapters 33 and 54 of Title 40 of the Revised Statutes.

Be it enacted *by the Senate and General Assembly of the State of New Jersey:*

1. The county library commission of any county or the board of trustees of any regional library established by 2 or more counties may, within the limits of funds appropriated or otherwise made available to the commission or board, purchase the following without advertising for bids therefor: (1) library materials including books, periodicals, newspapers, documents, pamphlets, photographs, reproductions, microforms, pictorial or graphic works, musical scores, maps, charts, globes, sound recordings, slides, films, filmstrips, video and magnetic tapes, other printed or published matter, and audiovisual and other materials of a similar nature; (2) necessary binding or rebinding of library materials; and (3) specialized library services.

2. The board of trustees of the free public library of any municipality or of a joint free public library may, within the limits of funds appropriated or otherwise made available to the board, purchase the following without advertising for bids therefor: (1) library materials including books, periodicals, newspapers, documents, pamphlets, photographs, reproductions, microforms, pictorial or graphic works, musical scores, maps, charts, globes, sound recordings, slides, films, filmstrips, video and magnetic tapes, other printed or published matter, and audiovisual and other materials of a similar nature; (2) necessary binding or rebinding of library materials; and (3) specialized library services.

3. This act shall take effect immediately.

STATEMENT

The purpose of this bill is to exempt county, regional and municipal public libraries from the necessity of advertising for bids in connection with the purchase of books and library services. In many cases bidding for such items is impractical; it delays acquisition of current materials and thus interferes with the library's function in disseminating information rapidly. In other cases there is no possibility of obtaining a discount from the list price through competitive bidding; and in some cases no competitive bids are obtainable. Since the purchase of textbooks has been expressly exempted from competitive bidding requirements in the school law (N. J. S. 18A: 18-5), the same policy should prevail with respect to public libraries.

Since Nancy Paige's findings were published in the *Library Journal* (15 February 1964), I have been told that they were used to good effect in many localities to get procedures streamlined. Hensel and Veillette's *Purchasing Library Materials in Public and School Libraries* has proved similarly useful.

A practical goal, then, for any library is a set of procurement procedures which does not impose any special paper work on the seller. The seller is paid on the strength of his own invoice and nothing more. He may be asked to put on his invoice the customer's order number, but he is not asked to render his bill on a form supplied by the library, or to have his invoice notarized, or to supply more copies of his invoice than is his custom. (Most vendors invoice in duplicate and ask that one copy be returned with the payment to help identify it.)

I have known libraries to go along with all of this *except* that they ask for invoices in triplicate or quadruplicate. I think the arguments against this are worth reviewing. Their reasoning is that the extra copies are needed, and the vendor can make them more cheaply than the library. They can also usually point to the fact that their regular wholesaler suppliers do not seem to object.

It is true that a vendor actively seeking your business and expecting your orders to average at least $200 per invoice, if not a great deal more, may readily agree to any conditions you may lay down as regards the method of billing. At worst, he goes through his regular routine and then carries the papers to a Xerox machine and works up whatever you said you wanted. He does your Xeroxing. It adds no more than (say) one-half of 1 percent to his costs, and he allows for that when he bids on your business. If his willingness to adapt himself to your paper work gives him business you might otherwise have sent elsewhere, he feels well repaid for humoring you. After all, you are paying for it.

The major disadvantage to asking for invoicing in triplicate or quadruplicate lies in what this implies about your own inside procedures. If you are asking for these extra copies, you are presumably using them. If you are filing one or two *more* copies of each invoice than other libraries, your costs are very, very likely to be higher than theirs. As mentioned before, the cost of filing a piece of paper once is about 10 cents, even if it is never thereafter consulted; the cost of pulling it out will be another 10 cents. The cost of filing two pieces of paper in two different places and later pulling them out again to match with something else will be something like 40 cents, even if they are then destroyed. If they are then refiled yet again, the cost of having originally required the vendor to give you these two pieces of paper may easily run to 60 cents.

Again, this may not be important on a $1,000 order. But it is not an insignificant sum on a $5 or $10 order. What appears to be an important difference between the acquisition of books and the acquisition of other kinds of materials is the comparatively high proportion of book orders that fall in the $10-or-less range. You can't ever hope to get away from placing a good many orders of this kind; it behooves you to develop a system that handles such orders economically.

Many years ago I worked briefly as a learner-volunteer in the book wholesaler house of Simpkin Marshall in London. Their procedures had been set up before the advent of the typewriter and the carbon copy—and long before the advent of the copying machine. Their systems were correspondingly simple.

The bookseller wrote out his order longhand, in ink. (Yes, this was still common when I was there in 1935.) Upon receipt, the books were picked and priced, the out-of-stock items were noted, the discounts were shown and extended, and the amounts due were totaled—all on the incoming order, or if necessary on a pasted extension of it. The priced order, now the invoice, was returned with the shipment.

You may say, "Ah, but they surely kept a record of the amount the dealer owed them." They did indeed. Before letting go of the order-turned-invoice, they slipped it between the moist pages of a large bound copying book. Thanks to the moisture and pressure, an image of the ink transferred to the semitranslucent pages of the copying book, there to form a permanent and chronological record of the transaction. It is hard to get things much simpler than that. On the other hand, it is basically unnecessary to get them much more complicated.

If, in fact, this proves to be the case, and you get only five or ten of the 60, you relax, and conclude that within the limits of human error your supplier's reports were probably pretty reliable. If, however, you order the 60 titles *and you get 30 of them,* then you sit up and take notice. Then you reason that if you had ordered the whole 600, you might have gotten 300 of them. That's too many wanted titles to miss out on, and it calls for a definite downgrading of your faith in your supplier.

In other words, the carefully planned spot check often tells you just about everything you could have learned from a total check — and at a small fraction of the cost. It has been accepted widely in both business and government as good accounting practice. It can be applied in many different ways.

For example, the Greater London Council, which is Great Britain's largest single buyer of books for schools and libraries, simply does not check every invoice (if it comes from an established source of supply) for the accuracy of its price extensions, etc. Only every twentieth invoice is checked. It is assumed (because experience has shown it to be true) that honest errors cancel each other out, whereas any continuing dishonesty will eventually come to light in the spot check. Payment is not even held up for verification of the delivery count; it has been found that this is an unnecessary step, inasmuch as 98 percent of the shipments do indeed check out, and in the other cases the vendors are more than happy to correct any errors that are called to their attention.

Such an approach might not be applicable in a situation where orders were large, infrequent, and often placed with a different (and possibly untried) vendor every year. That, however, is one of the ways in which effective book procurement differs most sharply from much other procurement, namely, that orders are kept small and frequent rather than large and infrequent, and large commitments are not made with vendors of untested reliability.

Take, for example, a case in which a vendor has delivered and billed a shipment of 50 books, but accidentally included a book which was not ordered. This is noticed when the shipment is checked in. The invoice, let us assume, correctly reflects what was wanted and what the supplier presumably thought he was delivering. Shall it be passed for payment or held up until the error has been corrected? Once the question has been stated, the answer is obvious. Pay the invoice as rendered. Proceed separately to correct the error. Any other procedure is simply piling paper work on paper work for no practical gain. Any slower procedure is simply unfair.

Any responsible vendor will correct any error, whether his or the library's, without question. He would never attempt to penalize the library for its honest errors, and neither should he be penalized for his honest errors, beyond (of course) being asked to correct them.

The process of auditing mustn't be allowed to get in the way of more urgent matters like the flow of books toward the readers and the flow of money to the supplier. He needs money to pay his bills, meet his payroll, and keep his promises to his bankers.

Once a supplier has "delivered" to the satisfaction of the order librarian (even if a few minor errors remain to be straightened out), he is entitled to be paid promptly. I have met city officials who would nod as I said this and seem to agree vigorously, and say, "Absolutely, we usually pay within 24 hours after receipt of his voucher." I say, "You mean his invoice?" "Well, no, we couldn't pay just on his invoice. How would we know we weren't paying it a second time? We have to have his sworn statement, accompanied by proof of delivery, that his bill is just and has not been paid."

They have lived with this system so long they are astonished at my astonishment. Only if the man I am talking to has himself had experience in private business will he understand why my eyebrows fly up, and he will add apologetically, "Well, I know that they didn't go in for all this voucher nonsense at General Motors where I worked before, but that's how it was when I arrived here, and I guess that's government for you."

This is hardly fair to government. It is true that a vendor has long been up against this sort of thing when he tried to deal with the New York City school system; but he has no such problem with the New York and Chicago public libraries.

Most public agencies follow the practice of the best private corporations. What the library is authorized to buy the library may authorize payment for. The outside vendor does not find himself trying to please several masters. The vendor has the responsibility for submitting bills that are correct or for making good on any errors, but the vendor is not responsible for preventing the library from accidentally paying the same bill twice; his responsibility ends with simply returning the money *if* it should happen.

Many of the difficulties in this area seem to have grown out of an overextension of the doctrine of dealing at arm's length. In the effort to give every bidder his chance, whether he is big or little, long established or just starting, systems are set up that would protect the city from loss even if the vendor proved to be incompetent or dishonest. In effect, all men are assumed guilty—permanently—on the assumption that anything else would be favoritism. Sometimes this attitude amounts to saying, "Why should we worry about the competence or honesty of our suppliers? If they don't perform, we don't pay."

This attitude is all very well where it is necessary. But it is like dealing with a bank where the paper work required to open a new account has to be repeated every time you try to cash a check. It's like being required to produce your birth certificate every time you order a drink in a bar you have patronized for the past 15 years. A far better policy is not to deal with irresponsibles at all, and never, of course, to deal with responsibles as if they were not responsible.

To be sure, if you place just one annual order, on a contract that is put out on bid afresh every year, you may be dealing for the first time with a stranger each time you write an order. Even so, if it is verifiable that his credit rating has been as good as yours for the past 50 years, it could be to your advantage to work along on the assumption that if he makes an error, he'll rectify it, whether or not he has been paid.

Toward Tighter Goals and Norms in Book Ordering Procedures

The library literature contains many a description of the basics of book ordering, but very little analysis and criticism. Such analysis as you find is extremely permissive. We could use a little less of, "But feel free to do it your own way . . ." and a little more of, "Look, stop being a damn fool."

It might be naive to think that any single set of procedures could meet all needs, but it is completely absurd to suppose that we couldn't study the hundreds of procedures now in use and boil them down to a handful at most. Perhaps we couldn't legislate the sillier variations out of existence, but we could go farther than we have to shame them out of existence, or surcharge them out of existence, or penalize them through slower fulfillment.

We might have hoped that the new form on which the Library of Congress now requires us all to order LC cards would have been developed as part of a total book acquisition system; in actual fact, it appears to have been designed with only LC's special needs in mind. Considering LC's power to impose its form on the profession, the design of the form could have been a long step forward. Instead, in my opinion, the new form is an opportunity lost, just as the LC card number (which should have been an ISBN from the beginning) never served any convenience but LC's.

Let's look at the new LC card order form. LC will supply you with single copies free of charge. You can go on using your old forms for your book ordering if you like, and type this one extra. But it's doubtful that you'll be very enthusiastic about that. It would make far more work for you than it would save LC. On the other hand, you've got problems if you try to make this LC card order form the top copy of your full set, because LC has monopolized seven lines of space on the card for its limited purposes, leaving you only nine lines for all your other needs.

Let's examine, point by point, the basic purposes of our traditional multiple-copy unitized book order form:

The *first copy,* the original, was for the book wholesaler. The key elements he needed from it were: number of copies, author, title, publisher, price.

The *second copy* was for LC or Wilson, as an order for the catalog cards. The key element LC wanted was the LC card number.

The *third copy* was for the library's own "on-order" file. It would be filed by author, and both filing and finding would be facilitated if the author information could be as close as possible to where it is on a catalog card, namely, upper left. Additional copies, if used, tended to be basically duplicates of the first (report form, claim form) or the third (temporary catalog card).

In this hierarchy of elements, clearly the *least* important element was the LC card number, since it would be used only once, by LC, and most of the other elements would be used again and again in filing, finding, checking, and so on.

So what do we find in the form which LC has now imposed on us? We find the equivalent of seven typed lines usurped by LC, solely to save itself the keyboarding of the LC card number, something which should not cost more than 5 cents at the outside.

Test this for yourself. Take a set of slips, say 20 or so, or whatever number you would normally send off to LC at one time. Sit at any typewriter, but imagine you are at the keyboard of one of the machines LC would be using for input to its computer. Keyboard first the number by which LC identifies you as a customer. Obviously you need type this only once no matter how many card numbers follow. Then type each card number. How long does it take? Perhaps about 10-12 seconds per number? Perhaps 4 minutes for the 20? Perhaps 50 cents at the outside in wages, fringe, and overhead to enter the 20-card order in LC's computer, or 2½ cents per entry? Five cents, perhaps, if everything is keyboarded twice—key verified—to prevent transcription errors?

Now let's assume you are given a choice. You may use LC's new form and pay LC's present card prices, or you may use your old forms and pay a 5-cent premium per set. Which will you choose? (Note, too, that the new sets tend to cost more.) It seems to me that LC owes us this choice, and it seems to me fairly obvious which way the choice would go.

The old forms give the clearest copy to the dealer, and who needs it more? The additional copies are *also* clearer, inasmuch as the first copy is on paper, not card stock, permitting all the carbon copies to be clearer. The old forms also give you *space,* precious space for all the other information you need to record, including status reports. The old forms are easier to file, easier to find again, easier to read, easier to annotate, easier on the dealer.

I wouldn't go so far as to say that the old forms we've been using are perfect. What the library suppliers have been offering are not so much the result of planned standardization as accidental consensus, "the way it's always been." The suppliers made it their business to give the customer what he seemed to want rather than to attempt to advise him on what he should want.

On some of the forms I have seen, you practically have to read all the fine print to learn the number of copies wanted or the list price, both of which are elements of far more importance to far more people than the LC card number. There ought to be a standard regarding the placement of each element.

On some forms you find at least the standard identification of author, title, publisher, in that order, but on others you find author, title, *place,* publisher. Now that's pedantry, pure pedantry. Would you really want *place* inserted before publisher in a tool like *Books in Print?* I think it would increase the length (and price) of *BIP* by almost 10 percent. To what end? And if not there, why on an order slip? For the cataloger? But nine times out of ten the information will simply come to the cataloger on the LC card, and in any case it could follow rather than precede the name of the publisher. (As a matter of fact, who needs this information on the catalog card, anyhow? The one patron in a thousand who cares could seek it in the book itself.)

A common failing of altogether too many forms is that no one ever puts himself in the place of the supplier or the typist. I don't say that no one has ever consulted the supplier or the typist. This may well have been done, without producing more than some equivalent of, "Any way you want it is fine with us, boss." The supplier is not going to stick his neck out and criticize your form; for all he knows, his honest comments would hurt your pride. The typist has perhaps never even heard of the science of motion study; she would probably reinvent it for herself if she were being paid a flat rate of 25 cents per form, or something like that, but she is being paid by the hour or the week. It is not her job to put herself in your place; it is your job to put yourself in hers.

If your typist were on piecework, however, she would soon tell you that any form is a failure if it cannot be filled out with both hands on the keyboard and both eyes on the copy—at least most of the time. This means that the place to begin writing each successive element should be findable through a tap or two on the tab key or a tap on the carriage return or some *simple* combination of both.

I have before me one "standard" form on which there are 11 different starting places in addition to the left margin. There should be at most three such starting places, and all of the elements common to most entries should be arranged, so far as possible, to minimize keystrokes.

One arrangement that combines some of the factors mentioned with consideration for the convenience of the typist starts the *author* information flush left, and allows a full line for it, then runs the *title* right on after the *quantity,* giving it a possible two lines but indenting any run-on by means of two taps on the space bar. The other information is presented either flush left or in one of two tab positions.

```
Delacato, Carl H.
(1) A new start for the child with reading problems,
      a manual for parents, 1st ed.
70-112380              McKay                    $5.95
Sep '70                8/15/70                  (Date rec'd.)
B&T                    (Classmark)              (Fund)
```

The chief advantages are: (1) The *author* is in the most convenient place for filing and finding. (2) The information needed by the dealer falls in the sequence he needs: *quantity, author, title, publisher, price, publication date.* (3) A full two lines are allowed for *title* and data related to the title, such as *edition.* (4) The LC card number is easily found, coming as it does flush left after an indent. (5) Data least likely to be typed at this time, such as *date received,* are placed in the last column, so the typist does not take time tabbing past empty spaces. (6) The least used data come last.

A small point, but one worth noting, is that no space need be allowed for the identification of each element. There is no need to let the word *author* intervene between the left margin and the beginning of the typed name; the words *author, title, price,* etc., if considered necessary at all, should fall between lines, possibly in colored ink.

All possible data will, of course, be preprinted on the form to save keystroking them, notably the name and address of the library, and perhaps its LC subscriber number, the code indicating what kind of a set of LC cards is wanted, etc.

Just in case this tab-column approach to forms design arrangement seems too obvious to warrant stress, let me show you an actual form which makes efficient (eyes-on-the-copy) typing almost impossible (see figure 1).

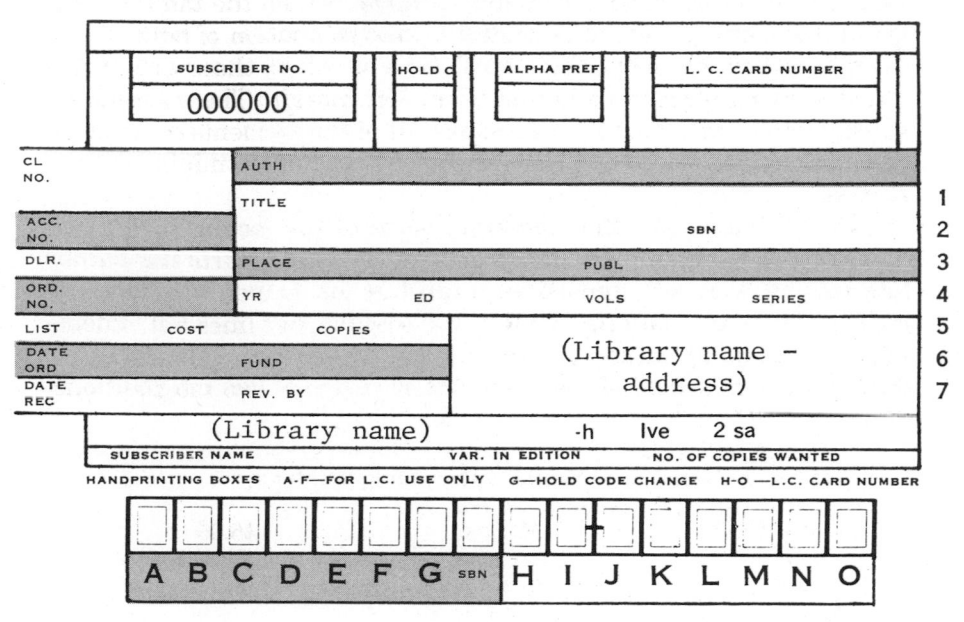

FIGURE 1

You may have noticed that in my tentative model I have provided for the LC card number but not for the ISBN. That is because I believe that the latter *must* replace the former. Technically speaking, LC should have no problem at all programming its computer to translate any all-purpose ISBN into a for-internal-use-only LC card number. There is no justification for letting a single-purpose number like the LC card number continue to clutter up our copyright pages and bibliographic citations when a multipurpose number like the ISBN is ready to hand.

LC should not only accept card orders by ISBN but actively encourage it, because then we'll all be using a number that will *also* mean something to our suppliers. To whatever extent universal use of LC card numbers helps hold down the cost of LC cards, so will universal use of ISBNs help hold down the cost of book ordering. This has already been proved in Great Britain, where the use of ISBNs has become standard.

31

Apropos of the single-purpose LC card number, I am not sure how many publishers would even bother to put it on their copyright pages if they knew how limited its use is. After all, how often do you wait to order the cards until you have the book in hand as a source for the card number? I am afraid some publishers think the LC card number is a sort of copyright deposit number, and some think it is a classification number.

Another element I haven't allowed for in my model is a purchase order number. I'd hate to see this used, because if you use it, presumably you plan to file one part of the form set by this number. But that would either duplicate your "on-order" file, which is arranged by author, or would be just another way of identifying the dealer. A big breakthrough can be made if you can get your purchasing people to think of each *slip* as an order, having as its order "number" the author-and-title information. Then your payments can be for any combination of these one-slip orders that happen to have been delivered, and yet-undelivered items can be thought of as unconfirmed orders that won't be confirmed until delivered.

I have provided no special place for *place of publication* because it is such seldom-used information. When thought necessary, it could be tacked on after *publisher*.

I have omitted the cost price, because lots of libraries do omit this, finding no compelling reason to go to the rather considerable trouble of posting it from invoice to order slip. I have heard it argued that this information belongs on the slip that forms the accessions book. But it has been pointed out again and again in the library literature that no library should ever *keep* an accessions book.

I have also heard it argued that one set of slips ultimately gets used to break down the overall book expenditures by *fund,* for which purpose the cost price is obviously necessary. Obviously? Some libraries just tot up the list prices and then take off their average discount. They reason that *exact* figures hardly matter—there are always many borderline titles that only a Solomon could say were more properly chargeable to a special fund than to the general funds, or vice versa.

Some controllers might learn to relax a little more when it comes to fund accounting if they could just be lent for a spell to one of the Community Chest operations. The managers of such funds cheerfully accept earmarked contributions from donors who are prepared to give only if assured that none of their money will go to some cause that is a pet peeve of theirs. Then each of the participating causes gets its full budgeted share anyhow, the non-earmarked funds being used to restore the balance.

In the course of preparing these incautious observations on operations I've never personally seen from more than one side (the publisher's side), I did dig into the library literature as best I could, notably Gertrude Wulfekoetter (*Acquisition Work: Processes Involved in Building Library Collections,* University of Washington Press, 1961), and I have referred elsewhere in these pages to the Hensel and Veillette study covering school and public libraries, and to the *Library Trends* issue of January 1970 covering research collections.

I was quite favorably impressed with Donald Dennis's *Simplifying Work in Small Public Libraries,* done in collaboration with Joseph L. Wheeler and Patricia Ann Sacks and published by Drexel in 1965 ($2.50 from Drexel Bookstore, 32nd and Chestnut, Philadelphia 19104). This provides some cost studies to measure yourself against and the methods for doing the measuring. The authors also come out strongly against keeping an accessions book. By contrast, Maurice Tauber (in *Technical Services in Libraries,* Columbia University Press, 1953) gives tacit approval to the accessions book by uncritically presenting, rather than evaluating, the ordering procedures used at Columbia.

I personally found it useful to study the procedures used at the Montclair, New Jersey, Public Library. Let me run through them here, since they are not only interesting in themselves but also provide a point of departure for a few other comments I would like to record somewhere.

A good many librarians are understandably reluctant to let an investigator study their acquisition procedures, out of a feeling that they'd first like to make their own private review, and perhaps tidy things up if they had the time. Arthur Curley of the Montclair Public Library was no exception, the more especially since his procedures were not even of his own devising; he had only recently come to Montclair and had inherited them. However, on my promise that they would not be held up as models (and perhaps also out of an impression that his predecessors had handled such things pretty well), he did consent to describe Montclair's procedures, by way of providing a jumping-off point for further discussion.

The Montclair Public Library uses Baker & Taylor as its primary source of supply, and has done so for many years. It spent about $60,000 with them in 1969 and got a discount of 37 percent. There is no formal contract or periodic bid-letting, though there was recent informal negotiation leading to an increase in the discount, based on a sharp increase in the book budget.

Suggestions for books to be ordered may originate in any library department and in any form. Whatever their source, they are first typed on four-part 3 x 5 order forms and searched in the main catalog of the library. If not found, the fourth copy (brown) is left in the main catalog, both as an indication that the book is on order — or at least under consideration for ordering — and to prevent subsequent duplication of this action. During this step the information on the order slip can sometimes be augmented from the main catalog. Note that typing the four-part order form *before* going to the main catalog makes one step out of what is often two. Some libraries check the main catalog first, then type the form set, and then have to go back to the main catalog to file in the temporary catalog card. Unintended duplication can also occur in the interim.

If a patron has requested the book and is waiting for it, the transaction is expedited; perhaps the book is even picked up by the library's truck from a nearby bookstore. (The library has found that this kind of if-we-don't-own-it-we'll-buy-it service builds enormous good will — and doesn't add even 1 percent to the book budget.) If no patron is known to be waiting for the book, a bit more time is allowed for cumulation and review.

The second part of the four-part order form constitutes the order. A month's orders commonly amount to about 1,000 slips, dispatched as one large monthly order chiefly for forthcoming books and several smaller interim orders for available books. As a rule, the immediately available books arrive about two weeks after mailing of the order.

Where it has been possible to ascertain the LC card number and enter it on the form set, the first copy of the set is sent off to the Library of Congress as an order for the catalog cards.

The remaining copy of the four-part set (the third copy, pink) remains in the acquisition section, filed under author, as its record of books on order.

The 3 x 5 order slip which represents the order is returned by Baker & Taylor along with the invoice and the book. If a patron is awaiting a book, this fact will have been recorded on the pink "on-order" slip, so that on arrival the book may be allowed to bypass the regular processing routine.

The LC catalog cards, if ordered, may now have arrived. If so, the set will have been filed behind the pink "on-order" copy. If it is apparent from the returned order slip that LC cards were not ordered, for want of an LC card number, the number is now ascertained from the book, and the cards are ordered. If the LC catalog cards have been ordered but have not yet arrived, the white slip in the book is exchanged for the pink slip in the "on-order" file and the book may be held in the acquisition department awaiting the catalog cards. When the LC catalog cards arrive and are brought to the "on-order" file, the fact that the slip is white and not pink reveals the fact that the book has arrived. Books awaiting LC cards are reviewed frequently, in case it seems important not to wait any longer and to proceed with temporary cataloging. Where shelfmarking is possible before receipt of the LC cataloging, notably in the case of fiction and biography, books are processed and shelved immediately.

In the ordinary course of events, about 600 books may be await- ing LC cards. Considering that incoming shipments average over 300 books a week, this is not a large backlog, though *some* of the books awaiting LC catalog cards may have been waiting for many months. (The number of books awaiting LC cards would be greater except that processing is often expedited by typing catalog cards from advance LC proofsheets.)

Every effort is made to identify books that Baker & Taylor does not stock, so they may immediately be ordered elsewhere. This cate- gory includes the publications of ALA, Government Printing Office, Wilson, Bowker, the textbook and encyclopedia houses, Peter Smith, etc. Otherwise, direct orders are placed *after* a title has been identi- fied by Baker & Taylor as not available from them. It is the intent and policy of the library to avoid asking Baker & Taylor to special- order anything not normally stocked, to forestall the extra handling that would otherwise be involved.

The acquisition operation is under the general supervision of the librarian who also handles cataloging, and under the direct supervi- sion of a nonprofessional, but experienced, assistant who has one full- time helper and seven part-time helpers, to a total of about 90 hours a week of part-time help. The duties of the acquisition staff include processing.

The library subscribes to the LC proofsheets. These slips, really proofs of the type from which the LC catalog cards will be printed, are weeded of items believed irrelevant to the library's needs, and then filed against the possibility that the information will be needed before the printed card sets can be obtained.

The library makes no demands on its suppliers with regard to the form in which invoices must be prepared. Baker & Taylor actually sends invoices in triplicate as a matter of policy, but only the first copy is used at Montclair. Invoices rendered in only a single copy, on the vendor's regular forms, without notarization or other added nota- tion, are completely acceptable and pose no problem.

Invoices arriving with the books are immediately checked with the shipment and delivery verified. Verification of delivery implies approval for payment unless there exists a large discrepancy between estimated cost and billed price — so large as to raise questions of serious error.

Payments are made by checks drawn on the library's own bank balances, normally no later than the fifteenth of the month following receipt of invoice. When the library's bank balances begin to run low, a request is made to the town for another installment of the town's budgeted contribution to the library's operation.

The only encumbering is what is implicit in the staff's awareness of its responsibility not to overspend. There are no problems about sending check with order to vendors who require this. There are no problems about making partial payments for partial shipments; vendors are not kept waiting for payment on deliveries actually made, pending delivery of delayed items.

Helen Welch, in her article about acquisitions in the *Encyclopedia of Library and Information Science,* observes that some libraries have as many as 15 parts in their order form sets. Presumably it costs them far, far more to handle all the resulting paper work than Montclair, with its four-part order form, spends. What do these libraries get for their extra expenditure? The plain answer probably is: Nothing really worth having.

The Montclair Public Library draws its funds from the town. The town is certainly as concerned as any town about preventing any possible mishandling of library funds: overspending, misapplication, and so forth. But the town feels that it has all the assurances that it needs under the present very simple procedures, and the record would provide no grounds for worry.

In some other library situations there is an enormous flow of paper from library to city hall and back. Bids must be let before orders are written. Orders, when written, must be encumbered and approved before being mailed. Every item on an order must be delivered or canceled before payment can be approved. The single typing that suffices to meet all library's needs is redone (often inaccurately) on elaborate special order forms to conform to citywide purchasing practice. Vendors are required to submit invoices in multiple copies, on special forms, notarized, and sometimes accompanied by delivery receipts. The only apparent provision for using sources which demand payment in advance may be to deal with them through another vendor who will accommodate the library in this way in the interest of having its other business. And where is the gain?

The source of the trouble seems to lie in the very real fear that someone will spend public money improperly. Clearly this must be a real problem with something like the construction of a public building. The builders need an ironclad commitment that they will be paid. The city fathers want ironclad assurances that no city department is making such commitments carelessly — and particularly that the year's commitments will not exceed the year's authorized budget.

The solution of the problem seems to lie simply in taking a closer look at the differences between buying buildings and buying books. You can easily afford to take $10,000 worth of precautions to make sure you don't pay $1,100,000 for a building that should cost only $1,000,000. You can't afford to take even $2 worth of precautions to make sure you don't pay $11 for a book that should cost $10. You must watch once-a-year expenditures more closely to ensure against overcommitment of available funds, as compared to spending that can be watched week by week or month by month. You presumably have to be very careful about irrevocable commitments to (say) road builders; they can't very well take the road back if you find you ordered it by mistake. You can be far more relaxed in dealing with a book wholesaler who will routinely take back anything ordered in error, whether the error is his or yours.

Could you go very far astray if you did all your encumbering of special funds only at year's end, what with the general funds to draw on where necessary?

Suppose the accounting office got no notification of any kind about orders placed — only the final invoices approved for payment? Is there, in fact, any commitment when ordering returnable merchandise? Doesn't it become a commitment only upon approval of the invoice?

Encumbering—Master or Servant?

In every system there is usually someone whose job is to prevent overspending at the close of each fiscal year, and someone else whose concern is to prevent underspending.

Shortly after I became a trustee of the Montclair Public Library, I found myself (in the presence of the mayor) taking the latter line. He said sharply, "Whom do you represent here, the taxpayers or the publishers?" I was trying, I guess, to represent the users of the library and asking only that we *do* spend what the trustees and taxpayers had said we might.

Coming out even at the end of the year ought not to be a problem. It nevertheless seems to be a problem in too many institutions, including federal government agencies.

The case for underspending is this: If you did your job and still managed to get through the year on less money than authorized, the taxpayer owes you a debt of gratitude, and you owe him the unexpended balance. Neither of you could know for sure, a year ahead, exactly what you'd need. You built in a little margin for error, so you could avoid the agony of going back for a supplementary appropriation. He let you do that, for the same reason. You managed so well, you didn't need the margin for error; so give it back.

This seems like a good system — always asking for a little more than you really think you'll need and normally turning it back unspent. The danger is that one fine year you won't *get* the leeway. Some hard-pressed budget maker, casting about for things to cut, will cut *you,* on the argument that you didn't even spend what you were given last year. From then on, you'll defend yourself, like everyone else, by making sure you spend every dime—or at least get it committed before whatever deadline you face.

Before attempting to solve *your* encumbering problems, it is important to understand what your purchasing officer may feel are *his* problems. His first problem is to make sure that none of the departments under his supervision overspends. His next problem is to make sure they spend the way they were directed to spend.

In this area there is inevitably a conflict between a library administrator and a city financial officer. The librarian tends to feel that if he overestimates his salary requirements but underestimates his book needs, he ought to be able to transfer some money from one to the other. He feels that if he underspends on books, he ought to be able to carry the unspent amount into the following year.

The financial officer may sympathize with these feelings, but he is generally far more aware of the abuses that can creep in without adequate safeguards. The librarian may, for example, have asked at last year's budget hearings for $25,000 for books and been turned down. His request may have been shaved down to $20,000. If it should turn out that he nevertheless managed to spend $25,000 by some juggling of accounts—perhaps out of a salary saved—the financial officer could well be taken to task for permitting the librarian to flout the expressed wishes of the city council (or the school board or the trustees or whatever) even with the best of motives.

Control of the details of public expenditure is critically important. It is easy to point to cases where money appropriated for one thing was improperly diverted to some other use. There has to be some control so that the holders of the public purse strings will not find that they have been conned—conned into appropriating money for a politically popular purpose, only to learn later that it was actually spent on something that would never have been approved.

In this context, the reasons for seemingly rigid encumbering procedures can be more readily appreciated. Nobody is really concerned about the possibility that you might substitute one children's book for another if the first proved to be unobtainable. What they are really trying to prevent is the possibility that funds approved for the purchase of books might be spent for some purpose that was never approved.

Another concern of the financial officer is preventing actual collusion and fraud. Book people and librarians like to think that this happens only in other areas, such as refuse disposal contracts. The financial officer, however, must consider the possibility of it happening *anywhere*.

He may ask himself: "If we give this vendor permission to make substitutions, how can I be certain that he hasn't slipped something to the order librarian in exchange for a private understanding that one thing can be 'bid' and something else supplied? How do I know this isn't like inviting bids on supplying the lunchroom with meat graded 'choice' and then letting the successful bidder get by with supplying meat graded 'utility'?" In most cases a frank discussion of these very proper concerns can uncover answers acceptable to all parties.

The analogy with the problem of buying meat for the lunchroom is perhaps a good one. Ordinarily an order for meat would not specify Swift's or Armour's; either would be acceptable, provided it was USDA "choice" or better. The lunchroom manager would not be required to state, weeks ahead, exactly how many pounds he wanted of the various kinds and cuts of meat. He would have freedom to adjust his order in terms of what was available, provided only that the prices charged were verifiable against some accepted standard.

The book order librarian asks nothing more. He says, in effect: "Under our supply contract I have the right to say that I want these 1,000 books at the bid discount, and the vendor has the right to say, 'Okay on 800, but the others are out of print.' Then, if there is time, I have the right to say, 'Well, then substitute these 200 other titles,' and he has the right to say, 'Okay on 160 of them, but the others are out of print.' Then I have the right to say, 'Well, then substitute these 40 other titles,' and he has the right to say, 'Okay on 32 of them, but the others are out of print.' If my patience holds, I can then say, 'Well, then substitute these other 8,' and he can say, 'Okay on 7 of them — one I couldn't get.'"

How much simpler just to say, "Here's my primary list, and also a list of alternates to fill in from if any of the first choices prove to be unavailable. Just don't exceed the indicated dollar limit."

As a rule, financial officers and purchasing officers *like* this solution to the problem, once they have understood it. It saves them trouble, too.

They may spot one hazard, namely, that when a supplier is authorized to supply (say) any 1,000 books from a list of 1,500, he will probably favor those which give him the best profit margin. This will be no problem if you are ordering ten times a year and give him this kind of option only on the tenth order, but it could be a serious infringement on your selection prerogatives if you gave him such options on every order.

A purchasing agent is necessarily a cynic. He is negotiating with suppliers who are pretty sharp traders themselves or they would never get a public contract. He cannot hope to be as expert in every line of business as his suppliers are in their specialty, so he relies heavily on open bids to ensure that they will keep each other honest.

(As one example of his problem: For many years one of the major regional suppliers won contract after contract by virtue of knowing more than his competitors, and more than any purchasing agent, about what the next year's purchases would probably be. This supplier would bid extremely low on items he knew from experience would be ordered only in very limited quantities, and he would allow himself a much better margin of profit on items he knew would be bought in much heavier quantities. If a purchasing agent then averaged the discounts, as if each item would be in equal demand, his would then seem to be the low bid, even though a weighted average would have told a different story.)

A purchasing agent's watchfulness cannot end, however, with the awarding of a contract. There is still the little matter of making sure that the contractor lives up to it. On a contract covering a mixed list of items, like a book contract, an experienced purchasing agent will not overlook the possibility that the contractor's margin of profit may vary from item to item, even to the point of giving him an incentive to wiggle out of supplying certain titles at his bid discount if he can.

His suspicions are not altogether without foundation. I remember in particular how one wholesaler used to win contracts by promising (among other things) to supply *Books in Print* at list price less 10 percent. Since Bowker's best discount to him was only 10 percent, and since he had to pay postage from his warehouse to his customer, he was obviously going to lose money on every order handled. To minimize his losses, he would supply as few copies as he could get by with. Somehow *Books in Print* was chronically out of stock with him, even while readily obtainable on direct order to Bowker.

A purchasing agent may well say, then: "Over my dead body will you let this guy off the hook on the stuff he contracted to supply. He promised to deliver; let him deliver. And we have the means to make him perform, because until he does we just won't pay." Unhappily this is easier said than done in the book field, for the simple reason that nonperformance would have to be proved on a title-by-title basis, and titles are often only $5 items.

In practice, then, the contract enforcement procedures which work well for pencils, or fuel oil, or typewriter paper are unsatisfactory when applied to books. A contractor can always get *some* kind of grade A, white sulphite bond typewriter paper, as good or better than what he contracted to supply, and can reasonably be held to it. There is just no way he can get a book that has gone out of print, and no way he can deliver a book within 60 days if the publisher isn't expecting the next printing for 90 days.

There needs to be a way to prevent a chiseler from pretending he can't supply what he'd rather not supply. But there also needs to be a way to enable an honest supplier to get paid for honest delivery and not be kept waiting until he can obtain items that are delayed through no fault of his.

In the general run of public purchasing, orders are for 3 trucks, or 100 gross of pencils, or 1,000 lengths of sewer pipe, or 100,000 gallons of fuel oil, or 100,000 copies of 10 basic textbooks. And then along comes the library and says, "We want 100,000 books, too, but they represent 5,000 different titles, from several hundred different sources. The average cost of the typical individual title may be about $4.40."

The prospect of encumbering all these books, title by title, is enough to make strong men blanch. It may never have occurred to your general accounting officer that there is a way out, but you might just put him eternally in your debt if you could show him how to get off this hook. And there are several ways to get off it; if one won't work, maybe another will.

Of course, the dimensions of the problem will be minimized if purchasing has been going on at a steady pace all year long instead of being bunched at the end. If you have $12,000 to spend, and you spend it at the rate of $1,000 a month, your year-end problems, if any, will be far smaller than if you waited until the tenth month to commit any of it. And, of course, you'll have the books earlier.

This works particularly well if coupled with a policy of having the vendor "cancel shorts." Presumably you will still want the shorts he cancels and the books he reports out of stock or not yet published, but anything canceled on this month's order can be added to next month's order.

Immediate cancellation of shorts is not the same as canceling shorts after 30, 60, or 90 days. However, immediate cancellation of shorts has important advantages and warrants consideration, though it presupposes that your vendor has wide and deep stocks of the kinds of books you order.

The advantages of writing "cancel shorts" on an order are many. There is one order, one shipment, one invoice. The vendor gets paid promptly, which will make him more than usually grateful for your business and attentive to your wants. You know immediately where you stand on the shorts and do not get money "committed" (encumbered) for something that may be a long time coming.

There is, to be sure, the problem of what to do about the titles your vendor doesn't stock and doesn't plan to stock, though he would presumably have special-ordered them for you if you hadn't said to cancel shorts. These titles must, of course, be identified. Clear-cut distinctions must be made between titles which are out of stock but on order, and those that "we don't stock and don't plan to." In the first case you can just re-enter the title on next month's order. In the latter case another kind of action is called for.

One way to handle the titles that the vendor has indicated he would have to special-order is to make them up into a special order to *him,* keeping such orders small so that he won't be too severely burdened by having to wait for his money until the last title has been rounded up.

Another way is to place such orders elsewhere, either with a wholesaler who does stock the books, or direct with the publisher. (As mentioned elsewhere, it is also a good idea to try the publisher direct on titles reported out of print. Sometimes you get them. And if it happens too often, you begin to wonder about the accuracy of your wholesaler's reporting.)

Of course, the practicability of a "cancel shorts" policy pretty much depends on frequency of ordering. If you are ordering monthly, an NYP title canceled from this month's order can be added to next month's order. A title which is TOS (temporarily out of stock) this month can be reordered next month. But if you are ordering less frequently, this is less practical. You might prefer the whole order were filled as (say) two shipments, those books that could be shipped at once and those that could be rounded up in the next 60 days.

There is no perfect answer. If you take what you can get in 60 days, you still lose what you could have gotten in 90 days or 180 days. And if you allow the longer period, you may be committing money to something that the publisher is only considering reprinting — and may *never* reprint. It pays to keep your supplier's problems in mind. Once he has shipped you a book you ordered, he deserves to get paid for it. And once he has special-ordered a book for you, he doesn't want to find himself stuck with it because you canceled before it came.

When you give him too short a period, he may even sit back and *not* special-order the book — correctly reporting it as out of stock but being less than candid about the fact that it will still be out of stock 60 or 90 days hence because he isn't doing anything to change the situation. This is all the more tempting for him to do since he may have found that special orders aren't profitable anyway. If you know or suspect that this may be his attitude, the best thing to do is handle shorts yourself and order direct from the publisher. At least you will know where you stand.

Under a "cancel shorts" policy, the question of whether you are encumbering by title really doesn't come up. You are, in practice, encumbering by vendor. If you are sending an order to Baker & Taylor for $2,500 worth of books, the important thing to know is that you have committed $2,500 of your budget. If your accounting office can know the dollar value of each commitment as soon as you make it, it can rest easy about any danger that you will inadvertently overcommit. Its job is watching the dollars; your job is watching the performance of the vendor. You commit (say) $2,500 for 625 books, then promptly learn that you have actually spent only (say) $2,000 for 500 books, and that the extra $500 is free again for other use.

Toward the end of the fiscal year, a common practice is to say to the vendor, in effect: "Here is an order for $2,500 worth of books, together with two lists, one of our first choice of titles, amounting to $2,500 worth, and one of some alternate titles, amounting to $1,000 worth. When you cannot for any reason supply a title on the first list, you are free to substitute one from the second list. Do not exceed $2,500."

Lots of libraries do this. Purchasing agents generally like it once they understand it, that is to say once they have satisfied themselves that it is on the up-and-up and is for the library's benefit, not the vendor's.

Yet another approach to the encumbering problem is as follows: Instead of "ordering" a list of desired books, just "inquire" about them. Ask the vendor whether he can supply them from stock and have an understanding with him that he will set them aside then and there until he gets your order. In this way, you will not write up the order until you are certain you will receive every book on it. Then write up the actual order for the books you know he has, and only those books. Once you get this arrangement working well, he may be willing to ship the books even before he has received your formal order, in reliance on the fact that he *will* receive your order. If it should happen some day that you were unable to follow up an "inquiry" with a matching order due to some unexpected cutback of funds — well, that's a risk he might be willing to take.

There are other approaches to the problem. Some libraries quite simply spend up their money well before the end of their fiscal year, and then in effect "go hungry" until they can legally begin to commit the following year's money. Their big ordering comes at the beginning of the new year rather than at the end of the old one.

Some libraries have a certain amount of discretionary money from other than public sources which can be used to bridge gaps or to guarantee commitments that could not legally be made out of public funds. Some, of course, simply take a relaxed attitude toward letting a certain amount of money go unspent, if it must. And in some situations, there is no real problem about letting this year's money carry forward into next year, or in swinging money from one budget to another; the power to do it rests with the librarian or with his board, and complications are minimal.

The Fallacy of the Bid Process

It is becoming increasingly recognized that contracts for the supply of books and related materials *should* be negotiated, not merely opened to bids. In fact, only 12 percent of the public libraries and 17 percent of the school libraries polled in the Hensel and Veillette study *Purchasing Library Materials in Public and School Libraries* considered themselves under any obligation to let bids, and a good many of these were probably reporting a custom rather than a legal obligation.

Considering that bid-letting is extremely common in other areas of public expenditure, it must be assumed that the reasons for making books an exception are persuasive ones. The basic reason which has moved legislators and administrators to make exceptions for books is simply that bidding procedures which may work well elsewhere *do not work well for books*. Wherever libraries have been required to seek bids and take the lowest, they have again and again found themselves confronted with flagrant nonperformance and no effective remedies.

It is not easy to see why this should be so, and therefore many librarians and purchasing agents have had to learn it the hard way, by bitter experience. After all, contracts typically contain performance bonds, penalty clauses, cancellation clauses — every practical provision for ensuring that the buyer *does* have remedies which he can invoke against a supplier whose service proves unacceptable. In the event of bad service, why cannot the library simply use these remedies? The reason is simply that adequate proof of nonperformance is so hard to establish. The typical book costs under $5, and proof of nonperformance has to be compiled book by book.

The custom of taking the low bid which held sway for so long was one of the inevitable results of applying to books the same city-wide or system-wide purchasing procedures developed essentially for other types of materials. The reasons for these procedures are not hard to understand. Those who spend public money have a problem that does not concern the private businessman spending his own money: They not only have to satisfy themselves that they are getting full value for each dollar, but they have to be ready on a moment's notice, or no notice at all, to defend every decision they make.

A bookseller can say to a would-be supplier, "No, thanks, I am quite happy with the service I am getting from your competitor." He is under no obligation to let bids or to explain whether his preference is based on lower prices, better service, or merely on the fact that his regular supplier is his brother-in-law. When public money is involved, it is *public policy* that the supplier who offers the best terms should not have to "know" somebody to get the business.

By far the easiest way for any government purchasing officer to keep out of trouble is to give each contract to the low bidder, relying on the penalty provisions of the contract for protection against any failure to live up to its terms.

The letting of bids can make good sense as regards the purchase of fuel oil. Shell's No. 2 fuel oil is presumably interchangeable with Gulf's No. 2 fuel oil. The amount of money at stake is presumably big enough to make it practical to exact contractual penalties in the event of failure to perform.

Since bid-letting has served him well in other areas, it is almost inevitable that a purchasing officer without prior experience in buying library books will apply it in the book area. Only after a few bad experiences does he back off and start asking himself why the usual enforcement procedures aren't working.

He may start by blaming the librarian for not documenting any failure to perform under the contract so that the penalty clauses can be invoked. The problem, of course, is in that "documenting." You can take a building contractor to court for failure to complete a building at the agreed price and within the agreed time, and he knows that you may just do it. You can also take a book wholesaler to court for failure to complete a book order at the agreed price and within the agreed time. But in this case he *knows* that you won't do it, because he knows that you would have to document your case on a book-by-book basis and if you gave your staff this assignment, it would have time for nothing else. It simply does not pay to do the research necessary to prove nonperformance on a $5 book item as it might on a $20,000 construction item (or a $5,000 oil item).

The building contractor wouldn't get far if he said, "Well, I've given you everything but the windows and the west roof and the heating system, but I'm having trouble getting those, so how about deducting those from my bid price and paying me off?"

Book suppliers, however, regularly say, in effect, "Well, I have completed 70 percent of your order, and I have had to cancel the rest because I can't get them, so please pay me for what I was able to get."

Is there anything wrong with this? Emphatically yes, if a more responsible or more efficient supplier would have delivered 80 or 90 percent of what you ordered.

The bid-letting system that works with construction and fuel oil and pencils breaks down with library books not only because proof of nonperformance is too expensive to compile, but because library books are, quite simply, *different.* The decision about whether to buy Shell oil or Gulf oil can perhaps be decided purely on the basis of price. Not so with the decision whether to buy Harper or Doubleday books. Books are copyrighted, unique, *not* interchangeable. Neither can the choice of wholesaler to supply those books be determined purely on the basis of price. At first glance a particular Random House book offered at 36 percent off list by one wholesaler and at 38 percent off list by another is the same book, and the buyer might as well get the larger discount. At second glance, however, this is not a case of two prices for the same book; it is a case of two prices for two different kinds of service, the book being the same either way. What must be compared is the service.

One example may help show how the low bidder may be the most costly source of supply. Let us assume that you want 1,000 books, having an average list price of $6, and that you are entitled under contract to get them from Wholesaler A at a discount of 37 percent. Wholesaler B had bid 36 percent, but lost out. Both suppliers must necessarily get the books from the same original publishers on the same discount schedule.

Five hundred of the titles are in high demand with all the customers of both suppliers, and consequently both suppliers are able to buy in large enough quantities to get 46 percent off list. Thus they can both buy your typical $6 book at $3.24 plus postage. One hundred of the titles are obtainable at 45 percent off list, or $3.30; 100 at 44 percent off list, or $3.36; 100 at 42 percent off list, or $3.48; 100 at 40 percent off list, or $3.60. One hundred are not obtainable.

Both wholesalers figure their cost of doing business at about 40 cents a book, which must cover postage from the publisher to them, postage from them to you, receiving, shelving, picking, packing, checking, billing, and miscellaneous other costs. Both would like to make a profit of at least 10 cents a book.

Wholesaler A happily buys and supplies the 500 books he could buy at $3.24, because after adding costs of 40 cents, there is still a profit available between his costs of $3.64 and what you pay, namely an average $3.78. This gives him a 14-cent profit margin. He also sees a profit in the 100 titles he can buy at $3.30. This plus his over-heads means his costs are $3.70—but he gets $3.78 from you. That's not the 10-cent margin he likes, but 8 cents is 8 cents.

As for the titles he buys at $3.36, now he has only 2 cents of prof-it. And beyond that he is simply losing on every title. To protect him-self from actually losing money, he simply elects to be (and stay) out of stock on the money-losing titles. They are in stock at the publisher, but somehow always out of stock with him.

In other words, Wholesaler A's bid of 37 percent never meant 37 percent on whatever trade books *you* wanted; it only meant 37 per-cent on whatever trade books he wanted to supply to you at 37 off.

Wholesaler B, however, took you more seriously. He figured you wanted every trade book you ordered, and he planned to get it for you, and he allowed himself more profit on the high-profit books so he could afford to take more loss on the low-profit books. Of course nei-ther wholesaler could get you the books that were genuinely out of print, though there *are* high-service suppliers who won't even tell you a book is out of print until they can report on your alternatives, such as a British edition or a prebound paper edition.

As Table 1 shows, both suppliers made about a 3 percent net profit on your business.

Your problem, of course, lies in those 300 titles you wanted but aren't getting. Let's say you are mad as a hornet and determined to do something. You reorder the whole 300 direct from the publishers, and you *get* 200 of them (at discounts varying from 20 percent off to perhaps one-third off, postage extra). You calculate that on average you are paying publishers' invoices to an average of about $4.50 each for books that Supplier A was supposed to supply at $3.78. That is 72 cents a book on the 200 books, or $144. Your contract gives you the right to charge Supplier A for the extra cost of going elsewhere to get what he should have supplied and didn't, and you think, "All right, *this* time we have him dead to rights, and *we'll make him pay.*"

TABLE 1

Number of books	Discount %	Cost	Cost—including overheads	Supplier "A"		Supplier "B"		A's profit	B's profit
				You pay	His profit	You pay	His profit		
500	46	$3.24	$3.64	$3.78	$.14	$3.84	$.20	$70	$100
100	45	3.30	3.70	3.78	.08	3.84	.14	8	14
100	44	3.36	3.76	3.78	.02	3.84	.08	2	8
100	42	3.48	3.88	3.78	(−.10)	3.84	(−.04)	(*)	(− 4)
100	40	3.60	4.00	3.78	(−.22)	3.84	(−.16)	(*)	(−16)
100	o.p.	−	−	−	−	−	−	−	−

*"A" takes no loss on these categories because somehow these titles are chronically out of stock with him.

$80 on $102 on
$2,668 $3,456
or 3% or 2.9%

As it happens, Supplier A pays, with profuse apologies! He doesn't admit for one little minute that he cheated on the contract. In fact, he is all injured innocence. Yes, he concedes, there may have been a few errors but basically your documentation doesn't prove a thing, since the books could quite well have been out of stock or out of print when he ordered them and back in stock or back in print when you ordered them. "Why," he might say, "you only got 66 percent of the books you ordered direct from the publishers, and you got 70 percent of the books you ordered from me! You never know whether a publisher will be in or out of a title in any given period."

You groan. You spent $1,000 worth of staff time getting the goods on him, and now he graciously gives you $144 and somehow manages to make you seem like a heel for wanting it. He has made every amends within his power, hasn't he? What can you do besides give him another chance when contract renewal time comes? Your purchasing officer, once he gets the picture, is likely to be your best possible ally, because although he has been taken by experts, he doesn't aim to let it happen twice.

There would be more high-performance wholesalers if there were more libraries willing and able to pay for performance as distinct from just paying for books. Librarians often say, "If only we could find a supplier who gave really good service—but of course his prices would have to be in line." In line with what? In line with the prices of suppliers who give bad service?

High service and high discounts are totally incompatible. Good service costs money, and the supplier who spends money to give good service has to get it back in the prices he charges. The only other way would be to let him charge separately for books and service, a possibility which is explored further in a later chapter, "Bidding on a Cost-Plus Basis."

This doesn't mean that competition between suppliers should not be encouraged. It merely means that the stress should be on service rather than discount. Service is far more difficult to measure than discount, but it must be measured in some way or it will deteriorate unacceptably.

Apart from the danger of getting high discount at the price of unacceptably bad service, another disadvantage of the bid system of selecting suppliers is the possibility of changing suppliers more frequently than desirable. No supplier can really do his best in a situation in which he knows he may lose the account altogether at the end of the contract period. Two- and three-year contracts are better in this regard than one-year contracts, but the best relationships are those in which suppliers are changed no more frequently than key employees. Ideally the reward of a supplier who has learned how to serve the library to its satisfaction should be relative security in the annual renewal of the relationship.

There must, of course, be some procedure for keeping a supplier on his toes. A very good way is to maintain concurrent relationships with more than one supplier, so that performance can be compared and good performance can be rewarded with an increasing share of the total volume.

In the past it has happened all too frequently that large contracts have gone to inexperienced low bidders who have gotten in over their heads. It would have been a favor to all concerned if there had been a policy against letting an untried supplier take more than a portion of any large contract in any one contract period.

Another important means of self-protection is to order frequently. Don't order just annually or semiannually; order at least monthly or, if possible, weekly. This way you learn what your problems are while there is still time to take corrective action.

Yet another defense against poor service is to re-examine your own procedures to see whether perhaps there is something in those procedures that makes cheating more or less inevitable. For example, if your supplier can't get paid for the books he *has* supplied until he has rounded up every other available book on your order (some of which are slow in arriving from the publishers through no fault of his), he will be strongly tempted to report the laggards as unobtainable even if further waiting might produce them. (See the chapter, "The Going Discounts," for other factors which affect discounts.)

The most basic step, however, is to adopt a policy of going direct to the publisher for any titles your supplier is not supplying. This not only gives you a line on whether your supplier is doing his job; it gets you the book, which is the important thing.

It goes without saying that you will be doing a certain amount of direct ordering from the publishers in any case, notably from those publishers who refuse to distribute through wholesalers. This includes encyclopedia publishers and others who normally give no discount to wholesalers, but it may include any others agreed upon between you and your wholesaler. If he doesn't stock certain lines and you know that, you may prefer to order direct just to save time.

Let's assume, however, that you are finding that your supplier isn't coming through with a significant number of titles that were well within his commitment and that you were able to get direct after he indicated he couldn't get them. What do you do next?

A good next step is to work up some estimates on what his failings are really costing you. Even if your library is fairly efficient, the cost of special-ordering a single title direct from the publisher may easily be $2 by the time you have paid for the form, filled it out, filed all its parts, matched them up with the arriving book, okayed the invoice, and paid it. In fact, don't be surprised if these costs run to $7 or more, as they almost surely will if you haven't set up special procedures for under-$10 transactions.

You may well find that the realistic costs of going direct to the publisher for a title your supplier said he couldn't get are as much as $10 above what you should have paid him under his contract. You may not be able to charge *him* with these costs, by reason of all the doubts that can be raised about how the title perhaps *was* out of stock when he tried to get it, or an honest error occurred, and so on. But you can weigh this kind of item against him in evaluating the cost of doing business with him. The cost of making up for his failures is just as much a cost of doing business with him as what you pay him.

You may find, of course, that your direct orders produce little beyond what the supplier supplied. In this case you might well decide to relax a bit and perhaps only spot-check his performance to ensure against backsliding. If, however, your direct orders produce more results than seems reasonable, then you need a better supplier, or at least you need to build a fire under this one.

Let's suppose your present supplier is delivering 70 percent of what you order, and when you reorder the missing 30 percent from the publishers, you get two-thirds. Let's say you originally ordered from the supplier books with list prices totaling $110,000 and expected to get (after elimination of the genuinely unavailable) about $100,000 worth, for which you expected to pay $63,000. Now let's say he delivered only $80,000 worth (at list), and dropped in your lap the decision on whether to give up (as he did) or try to get the other $30,000 worth. You didn't give up. You did try elsewhere, and you got $20,000 worth, which cost you about $15,000 in cash and about $10,000 in extra-order handling. Altogether, then, your cost on $100,000 worth of wanted books was $50,000 ($80,000 less 37 percent), plus $15,000 ($20,000 less 25 percent), plus $10,000 — a total of $75,000 for books having a list price of $100,000. Your effective, across-the-boards discount, then, on the books you wanted was 25 percent off list.

Suppose, however, you had dealt with Supplier B. In this case your contract discount was less, but the supplier would have delivered all the books you ordered, not just the books he wanted to sell. With him your effective discount (even if he wasn't perfect) would have been a lot higher than 25 percent.

It is hard to make these comparisons on a bid basis, of course, because what counts is performance, not promises. In the case cited, it is clear enough that you might have been a lot better off doing business with B at 36 percent discount than with A at 37 percent, but you can't be sure. B's performance might have been as bad as A's.

In such a situation there is a temptation to say, "All right, we'll put it in the contract. There will be a flat penalty of $10 against the wholesaler every time he says he can't get a book and we get it." I wish I could say that I thought this would work, or even that it might work on some kind of "5 percent deductible" basis, to allow for the inevitable percentage of titles that really weren't available when your wholesaler was trying and only became available between then and the time you tried. The fact is, I have never met a wholesaler who would even discuss such a contract clause, part of his reasoning being that you could start ordering things from him you never ordered before just to get the penalty money.

No, I don't think you're ever likely to get any satisfaction out of the penalty approach, any more than you can get "satisfaction" out of eating in a bad restaurant just by refusing to pay when the food is completely inedible. All you can do is stop eating there.

All you can do, then, is disqualify a supplier who has given bad service — and set up defenses against getting locked into another contract with another unsatisfactory source of supply. My favorite answer to this, which I have mentioned before but which perhaps bears repeating, is to deal with more than one supplier, and many libraries do just this. It helps keep each on his toes; it gives you a chance to compare performance; it gives you alternatives if, for example, one has a strike. It also provides a way to try out a new man in a small way, which could be to his advantage as well as yours.

In fact, there is danger in letting any large contract swing completely from one supplier to another between one year and the next. A supplier who has been giving satisfaction ought not to be dumped completely just because another bidder who is an unknown quantity comes along and bids a shade lower. Such an all-or-nothing competition means in effect that only giants — or fools — can even compete.

What is needed is more consideration of the problems of the smaller supplier. Set things up so he can take a small piece of your total business for a year. Then if he does well, give him a larger piece. A good general rule might be to require demonstrably good performance over at least three years before a new vendor could win the whole of a large contract. If he is low bidder the first year, give him a third. If he is low bidder two years in a row, give him two-thirds. But only if he is low bidder three years in succession should he have all the business. By then he will know what he is doing, and you will know what he is doing. He won't be jumping in over his head. More companies will be able to compete. And the bidder who finally wins three-thirds and then gets cut back to two-thirds will have time either to sharpen his pencil or to find other work for his employees. Suppliers who do a conscientious job shouldn't be changed any more abruptly than employees.

You may say: "Ah, but in our situation we don't have the option of working through negotiated contracts. We are compelled by law to let bids, and it would be impossible to invite bids and then to divide the business between the two lowest bidders unless the bids were identical."

All right. You may be as strait-jacketed as you say, though I wish you would first ask the powers that be to show you each and every provision in the state or city charters or ordinances that bears on the situation. I don't know of a single state where solutions haven't been found.

But let's say you must let bids. There may yet be nothing to stop you from having two bid lettings, one for each half of your total business, with a provision built right in that the winner of one will be disqualified from the award of the other. If this has to be specially justified, you will think of ways.

To help you make fair comparisons of the performance of both wholesalers, divide the volume fairly, of course. The cleanest approach is probably to divide by publisher: publishers A – L to one vendor, publishers M – Z to the other. It might also be a good idea to involve the suppliers in the division to prevent later recriminations. You might try the old cake-dividing technique: Let one supplier divide the publishers into two groups, and then let the other decide which group he will take.

The Going Discounts

As one of its services the state of New York, through its Office of General Services, negotiates contracts with several book wholesalers under which any library buys when placing orders of under $1,000 to be paid for from state funds. For the three-year period ending 31 March 1970, the contracts for long-discount books were with Richard Abel & Co. (30 percent), Affiliated Medical Book Corporation (10 percent), Allied Book & Educational Resources (35 percent), American News Co. (38 percent), Baker & Taylor Co. (35 percent), Book Fairs, Inc. (35 percent), Bookazine Co. (38 percent), Bro-Dart, Inc. (35 percent), Carol Cox Book Co. (35 percent), Charles W. Clark Co. (33⅓ percent), Cosmo Book Distributing Co. (37 percent), Dimondstein Book Co. (39 percent), E.B.S. Book Service (30 percent), Educational Common Market (38 percent), Educational Reading Service (34 percent), Charles M. Gardner Co. (33⅓ percent), H. R. Huntting Co. (33⅓ percent), Imperial Book Co. (33 percent), Key Book Service (30–38 percent), Lord Associates (33⅓ percent), A. C. McClurg (39.3 percent), Regent Book Co. (35 percent), Gerald F. Sutliff Co. (37 percent, and Taylor-Carlisle Book Co. (40 percent). Separate contracts were negotiated for short-discount books.

It is worth noting that the bids varied somewhat, but that all listed bidders were considered acceptable contractors. In other words, it was assumed that any library which considered itself better served by Richard Abel at 30 percent than by American News at 38 percent would be well advised to prefer the greater satisfaction to the greater discount.

No librarian wants to find himself paying more than someone else is paying for the same books and service, but on the other hand, neither does he want to find himself paying a little less and getting *far* less, or achieving small outside savings at the cost of larger inside expense. In the pursuit of the best balance between discount and service, and between outside and inside costs, the more he knows about the economics of the publishers and wholesalers, the better. (The economics of wholesaling are explored in detail in the next chapter.)

One anecdote may be appropriate. A few years ago the head of a small college library in a large midwestern city was comparing notes with the head of the public library, and noted that while they were both using the same wholesaler, the public library was getting a substantially higher discount. After an initial discussion of the possibility of letting the smaller library buy on the contract of the larger one, it occurred to them that perhaps the wholesaler would give even better terms for their combined business than he had been giving the public library alone, and perhaps better still if they could bring him on a single contract the business of yet other libraries in the city and state. They explored this with the other libraries and eventually with the wholesaler. He said he would gladly take on the combined business of the group—and could easily quote an averaged discount—but pointed out that while the smaller libraries would do better under the averaged discount, the larger ones would do worse! Needless to say, the larger libraries quickly lost their enthusiasm for the idea.

From the point of view of the wholesaler, the issue here was not just the size of a customer's orders, but the cost of fulfilling them. Some customers were simply easier to serve than others, either because of the kinds and quantities of the books they ordered, or because of the way they bought them.

Another group of libraries sought to increase their bargaining power by pooling their purchases. They found that they could indeed make their business more attractive to suppliers if they could combine six orders averaging one copy per title into one order averaging six copies per title, but only if the six copies were coming to one address. They found that the gain in discount would be heavily outweighed by the additional costs of first pooling the orders and then setting up a central receiving room in which the combined shipments could be broken up and redistributed to the participating libraries.

None of this should take anyone by surprise once he has taken the trouble to identify the various elements of cost that go into making up a bid. Since the wholesaler's margins must cover transportation from the publisher, transportation to the library, shelving of incoming stock, picking and packing of shipments, ordering and paying, billing and collection, warehousing, and interest on money tied up, each and every cost element must be pared to the bone if discounts are to be maximized. Only the customer who takes pains to save money for the wholesaler can expect the wholesaler to quote maximum discounts. Every cost created by the method of ordering must necessarily be reflected in the prices charged.

Factors Which Make for Good Discounts

Factors that help a wholesaler to quote maximum discounts include the following:

1. Ordering more than one copy of a title. It takes no longer to write an invoice for ten copies of each of ten titles than for one copy of each of ten titles, and it takes little longer for the warehousemen to locate 10 bins and pull out 100 books than to locate ten bins and pull out ten books. The motions are almost the same. In this respect, school and public library systems commonly get larger discounts than university libraries.

2. Ordering books that are in stock. Clearly it is easier to fill an order for a book that is stocked than for one that is not stocked. A stock of 50,000 titles might go farther to please school libraries or public library branches than a stock of 250,000 could possibly go to please college libraries or major reference centers.

3. Ordering books that are already published. Orders that are dominantly for already-published books will naturally be easier to fill than orders weighted with books about to be published. (As a general rule, school orders assay higher than orders from other types of libraries in already-published books.)

4. Ordering comparatively high-priced books. In terms of generating adequate operating margins, an order for a single $10 book is as good as an order for two $5 books. (This is where the tendency of the college libraries to order single copies, normally a negative factor, is somewhat offset by their tendency to order higher-priced titles. Of course this is less helpful if the titles ordered are not stocked or if they carry lower discounts to the wholesaler.)

5. Adapting the contract requirements to the wholesaler's capacities. It is far better to ask a wholesaler how he would *prefer* to handle shorts than to tell him how you want it done. He'll probably please you better if allowed to do it his way, because his way probably

represents a very careful synthesis of what his other customers have learned to like. This is also true as regards preprocessing.

6.   Accepting the wholesaler's normal billing procedure, without insistence on the use of special forms or procedures.

7.   Paying promptly for books received. The wholesaler who might otherwise be able to sell you a book for $3.60 will be justified in asking $3.67 if required to wait an extra 60 days for payment.

8.   Continuity in the buyer/vendor relationship. Really effective service is not to be expected from a supplier who must constantly worry about how he will keep his employees busy if this year's contract is not renewed. Wholesalers ought not to be changed any more freely than key employees.

9.   Precision in ordering. The customer who is *accurate* in giving correct author, title, publisher, and edition can save a lot of time and confusion not only for his wholesaler but also for himself.

10.   Fair play in giving the wholesaler all the business he was led to expect when he entered his bid. A bid is predicated on certain assumptions about the "mix," and it is not quite cricket to let a wholesaler assume that his losses on one-of-a-title orders will be made up on a fair proportion of much more profitable 30-of-a-title orders — and then send the latter orders elsewhere. Some of the publishers are actively seeking to take the "cream" of the library business and let the wholesalers have the skim milk. Where librarians let this happen, they must not be surprised if higher discounts from the publishers are offset by lower discounts from the wholesalers.

To get the best discounts, then, a library should first try to make its business profitable to the wholesaler. However, extra discount purchased at the cost of extra inside expense or inconvenience can be a bad bargain.

The Problem of Short-Discount Books

Trade books are only part of the library picture. Many of the books wanted will be "short-discount" books on which the wholesaler gets, and must necessarily give, less discount. It is an area where the integrity of the supplier is crucially important because monitoring his performance is extremely difficult.

There are entire categories of books legitimately in the short-discount category. These include elementary, high school, and college textbooks and many technical books, directories, library reference tools, and other books not normally handled by general bookstores.

Clearly a wholesaler can readily give you 10 percent off on the technical books he buys at 30 percent off, and perhaps on textbooks (at least the higher-priced ones) he buys at 20 or 25 percent off. Equally clearly there will be titles on which he himself gets only 10 percent or perhaps nothing (and even has to pay the postage himself). The danger is not so much that he will give you 10 where he could well have afforded 15; if he is expected to take the sour with the sweet, there must be some sweet. The danger is rather that he will take the sweet and hand the sour back to you, with the report that the book is "out of print" or "must be ordered direct from publisher." (It is true that the major encyclopedias and some of the H. W. Wilson services must be ordered direct. It is not true that the Bowker and Scarecrow publications "must be ordered direct," though no wholesaler could afford to supply them to you at less than list price.)

In a situation where a library's "mix" stays fairly constant from year to year, it is possible for a wholesaler to submit a seemingly simple bid, such as "36 percent on trade titles, 10 percent on others." This will leave him in the position, however, of hating to give you 36 percent on books he buys at 40 percent off and hating to give you 10 percent off on books he buys at 10 percent off or at list. Ideally the wholesaler allows for all this, and averages in the sweet with the sour and lives up to his commitment. He may protect himself against selling below his cost by providing for "special pricing" in such cases.

Libraries must allow for the possibility, however, that a bidder who has discounted himself out of a profit in the trade category will try to recoup in the short-discount area. He might, for example, cheerfully write his own definition of the "full-discount" category and limit it to the books on which he not only could but did get 46 percent or better, treating all others as short-discount items.

A university press once learned that its titles were being routinely billed at short discount by one wholesaler even though the wholesaler was buying them at long discounts, i.e., at upwards of 40 percent, depending on quantity. When questioned, the wholesaler argued that "everybody knew" that university press books were textbooks, and that textbooks carried short discounts. He added that, in any case, he considered any book to be in the short-discount category if he couldn't buy it in sufficient quantities to give him his 46 percent.

The library's problem is to know where it stands. It could be better to work at a basic 35 percent with a supplier who actually supplied most university press books at 35 off than at 36 percent with another supplier who actually supplied all university press books at 10 off.

Just how tricky this gets can be illustrated by the following story. I was once visiting a wholesaler of photographic books whose basic (and maximum) discount was 40 percent on five assorted. His best customer was a large library wholesaler who regularly ordered single copies at 33⅓, often sending five or more such single-copy orders in the same mail. The photographic wholesaler had helpfully alerted the library wholesaler to the fact that by just consolidating these singles into assorted fives, he could earn 40 percent instead of 33⅓. The response was, "Thanks, but if you will look after your business, we will look after ours." I surmised at the time that there was some internal paper work problem that made consolidation of orders impractical. It occurs to me now that this wholesaler might have preferred to buy at 33⅓ and sell at 10 in preference to buying at "long discount" (40) and selling at 35, and his contracts may well have left him only that choice.

Far and away the most usual common denominator of the general trade book is its availability at 40 percent off list in assorted quantities of five or more. It could be argued that any book is, properly speaking, a long-discount book if the wholesaler bought it — or could reasonably have been expected to buy it — at 40 percent or better.

By this definition, however, McGraw-Hill's Handbooks are perhaps a borderline case. A dealer has to buy 25 or more to get 40 percent. That should be no problem for a large, active, general wholesaler but is more of a problem for a smaller or more specialized wholesaler. Both would probably classify these Handbooks in the short-discount category, the former because the schedule on these books rises to a 40-percent ceiling, not a 46-percent ceiling. There might be some logic in a wholesaler's quoting one discount on titles supplied from stock and another, lower one on titles that had to be special-ordered — even when the publishers' discount schedule was the same on both.

The best source of information on publishers' discount policies is the *Book Buyer's Handbook* of the American Booksellers Association, revised annually and available from the ABA, 175 Fifth Avenue, New York 10010. It must be used in combination with the publishers' trade order lists as bound up in the *Publishers' Trade List Annual,* since only from the latter can it be determined whether a particular title is considered by its publisher to be in the trade, text, or other category.

Even with these sources at hand, however, it can be difficult to estimate what a wholesaler might have paid for a particular book. He might, for example, be in a special "agency" relationship to a publisher of technical books and be getting them on terms better than those generally granted retailers.

To make sure libraries aren't paying short-discount prices for long-discount books, some mechanism should probably be set up to help them know which are which. One approach might be tied into *Books in Print* using some method of coding the prices. I once explored with Joseph Duffy of the American Booksellers Association the pros and cons of putting an asterisk beside prices subject to short discounts. (Many booksellers are understandably reluctant to special-order a short-discount book for a customer unless he is prepared to pay a service charge, and they need some way of anticipating the problem.)

Duffy was keen on the idea until we came to the problem of trying to define exactly what the asterisk meant. Did it mean "subject to a 40-percent discount when ordered on the ABA's special cash-with-order Single Copy Order Plan (SCOP)"? Did it mean "subject to discounts at least as good or better than 5 assorted at 40, 25 at 41, 100 at 42, 250 at 43, 500 at 44, 1000 at 46"? The latter would be a widely accepted definition, but the publication of any such definition might have led to a reduction of discounts by publishers giving somewhat more.

We gave it up at the time. There are almost as many discount schedules as there are publishers. I now think we overlooked a possible solution. Many publishers include discount information in their annual trade order list, the one that goes into the *Publishers' Trade List Annual.* Why not just pick up whatever symbols they use in their own catalogs? According to this plan, if you saw a (t) next to a McGraw-Hill price, you could just look under the McGraw-Hill address to find out what a (t) meant to McGraw-Hill. (According to the *ABA Handbook,* a (t) at McGraw-Hill means long discount, (c) means 20 percent, (s) means 25 percent, and (i) means $33\frac{1}{3}$ percent.)

Although precautions of this sort are worth taking, they are really no substitute for the security that comes from dealing with a reputable vendor and assuming that it is in your interest as well as his that he make a fair profit. If a vendor doesn't make a reasonable profit on your business, you will get less than his best service, and if you try to beat him down, he may feel justified in getting back at you any way he can. And he may know more tricks than you do.

The Economics of Wholesaling

If one is to buy books effectively, there is no substitute for a good working knowledge of the economics of wholesaling. Such knowledge is almost essential if one is to be sure of getting a fair discount yet avoid making demands that reduce discounts unnecessarily or put the wholesaler in a situation where he must lower his standards of service to make ends meet.

A wholesaler quite commonly buys trade books at a discount of 46 percent and sells them to libraries at a discount of 36 percent. In the case of a $5 book he may pay $2.70 and charge $3.20. Out of the 50-cent differential he will pay transportation to his warehouse and transportation to the library customer, and he will pay to have the books put away in his bins, picked from those bins, wrapped, mailed, and billed. He will also pay rent, overhead, taxes, and interest on borrowed money. Hopefully he will also have something left for profit. If he were to try to work on the spread between 38 percent and 46 percent, clearly he would have only 40 cents on a $5 list price to cover costs and profit.

Assume for the sake of the argument that this wholesaler's costs average 40 cents a book. At an average markup of 50 cents a book (cents, not percent!) he will have pretax earnings of 10 cents per book — perhaps 10 cents out of each $3.20 of dollar sales, or about 3 percent of sales.

Someone may say: "Well, it isn't quite that bad. It has been some time since list prices of general trade books averaged as low as $5. On a $6 book, at the ratios given, he would have 60 cents of margin, and on a $7.50 book he'd have 75 cents margin."

True enough. And if he could get a school contract under which 100,000 volumes were to be chosen from an approved list of 2,500 titles, thus averaging 40 copies per title, his gross margin per invoice line could readily average $20. Nevertheless, the profit margins in book wholesaling are far from lush.

Consider then what sort of response a library might get if it went to this wholesaler, whose typical contracts are in the 34–36-percent range, and said in effect, "Come bid on *our* contract. Thirty-nine percent would probably take it."

At first glance, the wholesaler cannot conceivably be interested, since a quote of 39 would leave him no margin at all above costs. He might, however, say to himself: "If I had that extra volume, I could place bigger orders with the publishers and could hope to get a little more discount out of *them.* Anyway, the cost of handling one *more* book would probably be less than the cost of handling the *average* book. Besides, maybe this business will be easier to handle than usual; maybe their orders will average more copies per title, so the pickers and billers can cover more ground with fewer motions. I'd better at least talk to them."

At the talk he learns that the library will expect special invoicing on special forms, in a special sequence, that it is currently taking six months to pay duly rendered invoices, and that next year's contract renewal will again be put out on bid, and the award will again probably hinge entirely on discount with little if any reference to service or satisfaction.

He is no newcomer to library book wholesaling, so none of these things surprise him. Some of his other customers still think they need billing on special forms. The demand for special sequencing of the invoices is a bit more burdensome, since his procedures are set up for the sequence most commonly wanted by other customers. The problem of slow pay is serious. The publishers expect *him* to pay them promptly, and if he must pay them and then wait six months for the library to pay, the interest on the money he will have to borrow will cost him close to 1 percent a month. That could eat up any conceivable profit. In short, he investigates and declines to bid. He isn't sure he would want the business even at 36 percent, let alone 39.

Another wholesaler is less cautious. He takes the contract at 39 percent, on the well-established principle that the way to do business is to give the customer what he wants. This customer seems to want discount above all else, and discount is what he will get. He may not get all the service he would like, and he may not even get all the books he orders, but he will get the discount, which appears to be his only basis for evaluation of a supplier.

It becomes critically important to this wholesaler, of course, not to supply at 39 percent anything on which he himself gets less than 46 percent. Accordingly, any trade title of which he cannot buy the quantities necessary to get 46 percent (or better) is reported "out of stock." Since the contract provides for automatic cancellation of any title that cannot be supplied within a stated period, he has only to declare a title out of stock—and do nothing whatever about back-ordering it—and the mere passage of time will relieve him of the necessity of supplying it.

Obviously this is not living up to the terms of the contract. He contracted to supply all the library's trade book wants at 39 percent off; he winds up handling just the more profitable portion of its wants and letting the rest go.

Apart from losing out entirely on books that would have been supplied by a more conscientious wholesaler, the library finds that delivery of the other books may also be delayed. This is because extra discount can be obtained from the publisher by placing larger orders, and one way to place larger orders is to order less frequently. The wholesaler trying to operate on narrow margins can help keep his costs down by cumulating orders instead of filling them as received.

By these two tactics—failure to supply the less profitable items at all, and making no effort to deliver books promptly—a wholesaler can sometimes shave his costs enough to enable him to make the low bid and still make a profit. But he is still without remedies when it comes to the slow-pay problem. In recent years there have been several cases in which a wholesaler who wasn't getting paid as promptly as he had expected couldn't pay the publishers, which led the publishers to stop sending him books, which meant he couldn't fill library orders. I can remember receiving anguished phone calls from old friends in federal government agencies about Bowker books they should have received months before except that they had placed their order through a wholesaler who was many months in arrears on what he already owed.

Ideally a wholesaler should maintain at least a nominal stock of every book in print, or at least every book he is likely to be asked for. This would imply, of course, prompt replenishment of each title as it reached its reorder point. In practice, however, it is measurably more costly to be "in stock" on 95 percent of what you intended to have than to settle for (say) an 80 percent average. And to date libraries have shown little disposition to be willing to pay the extra cost.

Take, for example, a staple title which has been steadily averaging a sale of about three copies a month. It is not necessary to stock a large number since more can always be obtained from the publisher, probably within about 30 days. It might be sufficient to aim at keeping ten copies in stock, reordering when only five are left. This would mean that the normal reorder would be for five copies, which would have a fair chance of arriving before the other five had sold. However, this would be true only if the reorder were placed *promptly*.

In actuality, there is always a strong temptation to defer such a reorder to build up the discount. To repeat, a typical discount schedule is as follows:

1 copy	20 percent
2–4 copies assorted	33⅓ percent
5–24 copies assorted	40 percent
25–99 copies assorted	41 percent
100–249 copies assorted	42 percent
250–499 copies assorted	43 percent
500–999 copies assorted	44 percent
1000 and up assorted	46 percent

It follows that there is almost always a temptation to wait and cumulate orders, no matter how many are in hand. With 5 books needed, naturally one tries to build the order up to 25. With 25 needed, one tries for 100. Even at the 500 level, 1000 looks better.

The result is that scientific inventory control is overruled by scientific discount control. Even reorders for which customers are waiting may be held up to build discount. In present-day book wholesaling, a difference of 1 percent in the discount can be the difference between profit and loss.

In an effort to encourage more frequent "topping up" of inventory, some publishers have instituted what they call a "qualifying discount plan" under which the wholesaler who places a big stock order qualifies for the privilege of replenishing it at the same discount throughout the ensuing year. This is intended to make it economic for the wholesaler to reorder frequently so that he will be in stock more often on that publisher's titles.

But even if stock can be replenished daily or weekly without discount penalty, this is too seldom done. Conscientious inventory control costs money. There is an effort and a cost involved in making a buying decision and placing an order, and the *monthly* stock review (often pegged to the salesman's visit) is an established institution.

Wholesalers could be in stock far more often than they are, but any substantial progress toward really efficient stock control won't come until libraries demand it and find ways to recognize it and reward it.

It can be noted that the typical discount schedule tends to put the small publisher at a disadvantage. It may be easier to build up to a 1,000-copy reorder with the larger publishers than to a 100-copy reorder with a small publisher.

The wholesaler may say to himself, "Under 46 percent I just can't afford to handle a line." He has an *incentive,* whether he succumbs to it or not, to be chronically out of stock on the titles on which he feels he averages inadequate discounts.

This being the case, it could be very important to the survival of the smaller publishers—important to the very survival of a free press—for libraries to make sure they get what they *order,* not just what the wholesaler can profitably supply under the terms of his contracts with the libraries.

In the fall of 1969 one small publisher received a complaint from a librarian in Florida that her wholesaler seemed to be unable to supply his titles. She had grown suspicious because it did not seem plausible that so many of his titles could be out of stock so much of the time. The publisher was able to prove that scarcely any of his titles had been out of stock and urged her to order direct, which she began to do. In another case the librarian of a large city school system made the same observation and began a policy of checking up on her supplier by going to the publisher for what the supplier claimed was out of stock. Another small publisher with a line of special interest to librarians was stunned to learn late in 1969 that his largest wholesale outlet proposed to return 20,000 volumes for credit, in quantities that indicated a decision to cut back radically on the number of titles stocked.

It is unfortunately all too easy to imagine a financial man coming into book wholesaling—perhaps with experience in food wholesaling—and saying, "No wholesaler should try to carry every line—identify the profitable lines and drop the others." He would be right about wholesaling in general. He could be right about how to improve profit margins. But he would be proposing a radical change in *book* wholesaling practices in the United States, under which librarians have come to expect a "general" book wholesaler to supply all books of all publishers, or at least all trade books of all trade publishers.

It could be that the wholesaling of the future will move in this direction, so that you would normally go to Baker & Taylor for books of one group of publishers, to Bro-Dart for the books of another group, to Campbell and Hall for a third group, and so on. At present, however, you generally expect your chosen wholesaler to supply all trade books of all trade publishers, whether he likes their discounts or not, and to average in the sweet with the sour. Are we asking too much of human nature to expect a supplier to bid as if all books carried maximum discounts and not to lean a bit in favor of sending us the books on which he gets the better discounts?

Since time immemorial, wholesalers have complained about the discount schedule of any publisher whose discounts were less than the best. In the sales interview they will say to the hapless salesman (for whom it is illegal to play favorites), "I'll take 250. You think I'll need 500? Well, tell you what, if you'll send me 25 free copies for my salesmen, I'll tell them to get behind it and I'll take the 500." The implication here is that the wholesaler has the power to push a title on which he gets a better deal. Does he? Can he overrule your selection decisions and steer you toward the titles on which he makes the most? Of course he hasn't *got* 25 salesmen — at least not selling books on a title-by-title basis — and all he will do with the extra 25 copies is add them to his stock, thus netting in effect several extra points of discount. But he may have more power to sway your selection decisions than you think. (See also "Book Selection — How Publishers Influence It, or Try To," page 100.)

Of course it might be argued that the more your wholesaler can get from the publishers the more discount he can give you, so that in effect he is waging your battle. Unhappily there are side effects. The publisher who has been pricing at $10, giving 46 percent off, and "getting by" may just have to reprice at $11 if crowded up to 50-percent discount. If he is unable to do this by reason of resistance in retail channels, he may even go out of business and reduce by that much the range of choice open to you. The worst effect, however, is the infringement on your selection prerogatives. Once you have made a book selection decision, you do not want to find out months later that your wholesaler overruled you because he wanted 10 cents more discount than the publisher was offering.

There should be an answer to this problem, one that would remove the wholesaler's incentive to switch you. Such an answer could be the "cost-plus" contract, examined more fully in the next chapter.

It is noteworthy that the very items which one wholesaler prefers not to handle at all may be the stock-in-trade of a more specialized wholesaler. Some wholesalers feel they can't afford to handle paperbacks; A & A handles nothing else. Some wholesalers handle medical books only on a special-order basis, but firms like Eliot Books, Brown

& Connolly, and Chicago Medical happily stock them. Some whole-salers make no effort to fill orders for titles not found in *Books in Print;* Richard Abel, however, routinely accepts and fills orders for titles of foreign origin.

Each order librarian must allow for this kind of limitation and specialization in setting up his lines of supply. If he can find a single source of supply ready, willing, and able to supply all his needs in every category, well and good. More typically, however, he ends by setting up several lines of supply. One large public library orders its trade books from Baker & Taylor, its paperbacks from A & A, its pamphlets from the Bacon pamphlet service, its British books from Blackwell, and so on. It also places many orders direct with the pub-lisher. Titles reported unobtainable by a wholesaler are routinely reordered direct from the publisher just to make sure. The guiding principle is, "Get all the discount you can—but get the book regard-less. We are buying books, not discount." Needless to say, many items carry no discount at all, notably pamphlets, association publications, documents, and the like, and on occasion the supplier is fully justified in charging list price plus a service fee.

Bidding on a Cost-Plus Basis

At present the wholesaler who buys at 46 and sells at 36 makes a 10-percent spread on the list price which amounts to 10 cents on a $1 book, 30 cents on a $3 book, 50 cents on a $5 book, 60 cents on a $6 book, $1 on a $10 book, etc. It is obvious that nobody can buy, store, pick, pack, and invoice a $1 pamphlet for a 10-cent service charge; no wonder that as a practical matter book wholesalers hate to carry pamphlets or low-priced books or short-discount books or lots of other things that you'd happily buy from them if you could and which you are now being forced to buy elsewhere at a surcharge (in inside effort or money) probably higher than an outside supplier might have charged.

Why doesn't the wholesaler simply charge you his cost plus his service charge and stop worrying about whether he can "afford" to carry low-priced or short-discount items? Up to now comparatively few wholesalers have done this because they believe, rightly or wrongly, that if they proposed (say) a $1 surcharge for getting you a 50-cent pamphlet, you would be outraged, even if your alternative was to go through your full internal purchase order routine at several times that cost.

They believe, probably with much justification, that their average customer simply doesn't stop to calculate how much extra it costs him to place a lot of direct-to-publisher orders in place of one direct-to-wholesaler order. Their typical customer reasons (they feel) as follows: "We already have the staff. Writing one more requisition, approving one more purchase order, checking in one more shipment, okaying one more bill, writing one more check—such extra work can be absorbed."

This customer does not stop to say to himself, "Ah, but isn't this insidious absorption process what necessitated our last staff increase? Even if we could absorb 100 such extra transactions per month without visible extra outlay, what if the 101st was the straw that broke the camel's back and committed us to another $500 a month in salaries and fringe and overhead? In this case wouldn't it have been better to think as if each and every one of the past 100 increments to our work load had cost us $5?"

Wholesalers are confident that your inside costs of making a direct purchase will always be higher than anything they'd have to charge you for just adding the item to your regular purchase order—but they aren't sure you recognize this. They aren't sure you *know* your inside costs.

There is another reason why some wholesalers are reluctant to talk about transaction costs as distinct from discounts. If they were to say too much about how their costs average, at least so much per book, or so much per "line item" on the invoice (which often involves two or more copies of one title), you might come back at them and note that at present they often get more than this. When they are working on the difference between 36 and 46 on a $5 book, their margin may be only 50 cents, but when they have the same 10-point spread on a $50 book (or five copies of a $10 book), they have $5. You might say, "If we give you more on the low-priced items, how about taking less on the high-priced ones?" What the wholesaler obviously fears is that he might come out of any such discussion with no more margin on the least profitable items and somewhat less on the others.

Wholesalers used to complain about not getting enough discount on *Books in Print*. Some refused to handle it on that ground. Yet because of its comparatively high net price it gave them, at 10 percent discount, substantially more than they were getting on their average line item.

It can be argued that a wholesaler is so often expected to handle small units at a loss that he ought to be allowed to make up these losses through comparatively large profits on higher priced units. In theory, a contractual discount, such as 36 percent off list on general trade books, is supposed to represent an averaging out of the sour with the sweet. In practice, some libraries write such a contract and then start skimming off the cream. They start ordering direct on $50 items on which the wholesaler could really have made a profit, and

71

the wholesaler in turn starts trying to get out of handling anything that gives him less than he thinks just.

It could be far better for everyone if these incentives to cut corners could be eliminated. It could be far better if every tub could stand on its own bottom.

Those who advocate working on a "cost plus service charge" basis, e.g., wholesaler's cost plus certain flat charges geared to units, line items, invoices, and dollar totals, cite the following advantages:

1. A wholesaler would be guaranteed an agreed margin of profit on every item, regardless of whether it carried a discount to him of 50 percent, 46, 43, 40, 33, 25, 10, or nothing, and regardless of whether it was priced at $10, $5, or even $1.

2. He could order and replenish solely with an eye toward *having* in stock what he intended to have, without concern for holding back reorders to build discount. To be sure, this policy would probably show up on your invoice as a slightly higher "cost," but there isn't a cost accountant in the business who wouldn't back you up if you argued that *getting* a book is *worth* a little more than learning that you aren't going to get it unless you go direct to some obscure publisher.

3. Stress would be back on service where it belongs.

What are the arguments *against*? What the major wholesalers *say* is that they don't think libraries would go for this plan, though they grant that it is possible.

Certainly there is also a certain reluctance to *reveal* their costs. Few businessmen would react otherwise. They would say (or at least think), "My costs are none of your damn business." They would reason, "If my customer knew my costs, he would press me much harder for price concessions."

This is natural, but really irrelevant. What the book wholesalers pay the publishers is public knowledge. At least the publishers' list prices are certainly public knowledge, and the publishers' discount schedules are accessible to any librarian who cares to purchase the annual *Handbook* of the American Booksellers Association.

It can be argued that even a computer could hardly keep up with true per-title costs. An original quantity might be bought at 48 percent off, and subsequent reorders at 46, 43, or anything. Transportation is a cost and varies from shipment to shipment.

This can all be worked out. One way would be to consider that every title in stock had cost what the most recent reorder had cost. Another would be to assume that transportation costs would be directly proportional to book cost. Such assumptions could be corrected from time to time in the light of actual experience.

It could be argued that a flat service fee — $1 a volume, for example — while it might be fine for some books, would be too small to cover the cost of handling an expensive book, inasmuch as expensive books tend to take up more space and tie up more capital. Very well. Let the wholesaler base his service charge *partly* on the number of volumes picked and partly on the cost price of these volumes. If he liked, he could even work in additional factors: for example, 20 cents per volume, plus 20 cents per invoice line, plus 10 percent of the cost price, the latter inclusive of a factor for transportation.

Any computer would make light work of such a calculation. Each invoice could end with a "service charge" based on so many volumes, so many invoice lines, and so much dollar total. If desired, a flat "per-order" amount (such as $2) could be added to make it immaterial to the wholesaler whether the business came as a few large orders or as many small ones directed to many addresses.

There should be an agreement that invoices for books shipped (even if only part of an order) are due and payable within 30 days from the end of the month in which rendered, with a surcharge of 1 percent a month for any delay. (There could be an understanding that payments made prior to verification of delivery could be renegotiated.)

It could be argued that such a scale of charges would not adequately cover the wholesaler for special-ordering items not stocked. This is true enough and should probably be covered in some way, perhaps through mutual understanding of the lines the wholesaler *does* propose to stock and a surcharge for obtaining books from other sources.

Other problems would surely have to be worked out or averaged out. It is not suggested that the wholesaler should be reimbursed in the service charge for certain itemized costs and *not* reimbursed for others not itemized, but rather that he should carefully calculate his overall costs, build in an allowance for profit, and then construct a formula to cover everything. The advantage of charging some costs by the number of volumes picked, some by the invoice line, some in proportion to dollar costs, and some in proportion to the number of shipments is that this kind of allocation, if carefully worked out, could eliminate undesirable incentives — most notably, the present reluctance to handle the less profitable items.

How to Buy Paperbacks

Most of the problems in book acquisition seem to arise out of mistaken identity—trying to buy books by bid procedures really devised for fuel-oil contracts, trying to buy trade books by methods really applicable only to textbooks, or trying to buy paperbacks by methods really applicable only to hardbounds. All of these are too different one from another to permit this kind of impartiality.

We all recognize the differences when we must. We use scrip or set up a deposit account if we want paperbacks from the U.S. Government Printing Office. We order LC catalog cards by LC catalog card numbers. We buy our low-priced sundries at cash-and-carry chain stores and do not expect a big department store to give us "charge-and-deliver" service on a box of Kleenex. If we want some Kayser hosiery, we go to a merchant who carries this line; we don't expect another merchant to special-order it for us.

We would do well to remember all this when we try to buy paperbound books, because many paperbacks are merchandise first and books only incidentally. They move through the same channels as newsstand merchandise. They sell alongside cigarettes and camera film. They have to be handled on the same kind of profit margins as candy or toys. They cannot be thought of as just books that don't have hard bindings; they are an entirely different breed of cat. There are basically three kinds: the so-called mass-market titles, the higher-priced (class) titles, and the short-discount (textbook) titles.

There are about 30 active mass-market publishers, issuing between them about 300 new titles a month, and fighting it out for a showing of these new titles in the 100 or so pockets in the typical newsstand outlet. This month's new titles, plus last month's, plus the staples are carried into the newsstands and drugstores by 600 local news wholesalers, each with what might be called a "truck-loop" territory. A few carry deeper stocks, but not many, and usually a bookstore attempting to carry more than a few hundred paperbacks must deal directly with the publishers or with one of the few active full-line paperback wholesalers.

Outside the mass-market area, the "class" paperbacks behave somewhat more like hardbounds, except that the markups make them harder to handle at a profit. Most of these (unlike the mass-market titles) are printed on paper which will not turn yellow and brittle in a few years. Often they have margins generous enough to permit sewing into a Class A library binding.

Then there are the short-discount titles, which the publisher is primarily interested in selling for class adoptions, and a certain number of no-discount titles, such as the *Literary Market Place*.

Far and away the easiest way to buy the lower-priced paperbacks would be to buy exactly as your local newsstand does. Let his wholesaler service you from the same truck, on the same schedule. That truck will bring you, with full return privileges, a full assortment of each month's new mass-market titles, some 300–400 of them, sweetened up with staples like Spock and the *Pocket Dictionary*. And it will take away what hasn't "sold." Such a local news wholesaler will operate on about a 40-percent margin and let you have 20 percent.

He may or may not stand ready to service you with the higher-priced paperbacks; most probably he will not. But if you were operating a full-scale paperback bookstore, you would make your arrangements to get these from another kind of wholesaler, such as A & A near Boston. Of course, if you had a store big enough to be self-sufficient, you'd be moving several hundred books a week, so there'd be a good many titles per order and per invoice.

You may say, however, that this wouldn't be your pattern. You don't sell paperbacks, and you don't buy many. Whereas the wholesalers who serve retailers live by frequent orders for high quantities of a limited number of titles, you as a library are much more likely to place infrequent orders for low quantities (even singles) of an unlimited number of titles.

In fact, many libraries order paperbacks only when no hardbound edition is available, and often need only a single copy of a single title priced at $2 or less, preferably from a supplier who will bill them — and give a discount. They are surprised to find that no one — neither wholesaler nor publisher — really wants such orders, with or without discount. Oh, the publishers are glad enough to have orders for heavy quantities from a school system using paperbacks as textbooks or for classroom libraries. They don't refuse orders for 25s and 50s. But *no one* welcomes small orders for editions priced at $2 or less, at least not if the buyer wants to be billed.

This means that when you want one of the 88,000 paperbacks of the 1,500 publishers listed in *Paperbound Books in Print*, you have your work cut out for you. Even A & A, who have the most complete stock of paperbacks, may not have more than 40,000 titles of 300 publishers in stock. The best paperback bookstore you ever saw probably didn't have more than 10,000. And it would be remarkable if your local news wholesaler had as many as 2,000.

Furthermore, many of the 1,500 publishers of those 88,000 titles didn't have you in mind at all when they planned their distribution. Some won't even *acknowledge* an order for a single copy unless it comes with a check for full list price plus postage or a handling charge.

You might suppose that the publisher of a paperback textbook who normally makes a wide distribution of free sample copies in an effort to get adoptions would be only too glad to get paid for one of these samples and have it lodged in a library where it might be seen by any number of potential adopters not on his free list. Forget it. When the publisher's aim is selling adoption quantities, you'd probably have better luck requesting a free desk copy on some educational stationery than trying to get one by paying.

Other paperbacks are sometimes created primarily as subscription premiums or for free distribution to a membership list. Selling them to libraries, one at a time, the way ALA sells its publications to libraries, just isn't part of the picture. Some of the publishers listed in *Paperbound Books in Print* wish they hadn't been. Some of the textbook publishers used to stay out of the *Publishers Trade List Annual* and *Books in Print* expressly to avoid the bother of receiving single-copy orders.

Libraries do need a good wholesale source for the paperbacks they can't buy locally. I have a letter from a librarian who says, "I can sympathize with the problems faced by the paperback wholesalers, *but we need this service.*" That's fine, but it's not enough. The question is whether enough libraries need such service *enough* — enough to pay whatever it would cost to make it economic.

In past years there has been a high mortality rate among would-be paperback wholesalers, but there are still several wholesalers carrying wide and deep stocks of paperbacks, one in New England, two in the Middle West, one in the Rocky Mountain area. Their services are available to libraries, but they depend for their economic survival on serving retailers who know the value of a dollar and don't expect them to fill single-copy orders, bill on special forms, notarize invoices, submit sealed bids, or post performance bonds.

They could — and no doubt they *do* when the quantities are high enough — give libraries extra service at extra cost. But a far better way to deal with them is on their own terms. It isn't a concession, it's a privilege, because they are actually demonstrating how books can be handled at about half the conventional cost. If you have had bad luck trying to work with some of them, consider the possibility that they'd like to be cooperative, but they owe their very existence to a policy of cutting costs to the bone, and to them billing a single paperback is about as sinfully and senselessly wasteful as touching a match to a dollar bill.

They are not alone in this commitment to watching the pennies. No less an agency than the U.S. Government Printing Office takes much the same attitude because it has much the same problems. The Superintendent of Documents is just as committed as the paperback wholesalers to keeping his costs down, and he has an advantage that is denied to the wholesalers in that he can set his own prices and is not at the mercy of a publisher who suddenly decides to shorten his discounts.

The way to get the maximum of help from a paperbound wholesaler like A & A is to start by putting yourself in his shoes. If you were A & A, you wouldn't be very enthusiastic about filling and billing an order for one paperback. In fact, you'd probably move promptly to a policy much like that of Sudox — cash in advance and no discounts. You might even decide to charge a flat $2 or so for any bill rendered, above and beyond the price of the books. (Not that A & A does this, but you might in A & A's shoes.)

You would find you could not possibly afford to get involved in back-ordering, so you'd supply what was on the shelf and report the rest unavailable. If you found that the publishers and booksellers liked to work by number instead of titles, you also would find yourself shelving, picking and billing, and replenishing stock by title number (not very different, really, from what LC requires of its catalog card customers), and you would be unenthusiastic when a library customer asked you to bill by author and title. *And* you might be less than happy if you found that a customer was sending the cream of his business elsewhere and giving you just the dregs.

After all, if your regular hardbound wholesaler doesn't carry the paperbacks you want, there's a reason: He doesn't see how he can do so at a profit. At least, he can't do it and still give you the service you expect of him on the hardbounds. If you then take your paperback business — which your regular wholesaler didn't want, remember — to another wholesaler, your problem is not which other wholesaler will give you the best discount. Your problem is finding one who will serve you at all.

If it normally costs you $2 or more to place an order and pay for it, and normally costs your hardbound wholesaler another $2 to fill the order and bill it, this is obviously no way to buy a single copy of a $2 paperback. To make ends meet, he'd have to bill you at list price plus a $2 service charge, and the $2 paperback would wind up costing you more nearly $6.

The best way to buy almost any low-priced product is on a self-service, cash-and-carry basis. Just walk into Woolworth's or the supermarket or the drugstore and pick it up. And this self-service, cash-and-carry basis is probably the best way of buying paperbacks, too, if you are lucky enough to be near a bookstore or college store with a good selection. However, no retailer will have more than a fraction of the titles in *Paperbound Books in Print*, so you'll have to do some ordering by mail.

Unfortunately, your regular source of hardbounds won't have many paperbacks, either — probably fewer (if any) than your nearest college store. The wholesaler doesn't like to carry them because if he gives you the kind of discounts and service you expect, he loses money, and if he charges enough to cover his costs, many of his customers get angry with him because they think he is gouging. (The exception here is the prebinder of paperbacks, who can make his money on the binding if not on the book itself.)

Where you can't get a low-priced product on a self-service, cash-and-carry basis, the next best thing is to come as close as you can on a mail-order basis, i.e., order by *number* (this is self-service of a sort — it saves the supplier from looking up the number) and send cash in advance to avoid the costs of billing. This is the way you order government documents, LC catalog cards, and most mail-order merchandise.

For the majority of the 88,000 paperbacks listed in *Paperbound Books in Print*, you'll have to send direct to the publisher, and unless you like aggravation better than results, send cash with order at the full list price plus postage. If the Superintendent of Documents, who is a specialist in supplying single copies of paperbound material by mail, won't give you a discount or bill you, you can hardly expect this kind of service from a private publisher who probably isn't set up to fill single-copy orders at all.

Although your regular hardbound wholesaler may not be much help on paperbacks, there are, as mentioned earlier, a few wholesalers specializing in paperbacks. Let's take a look at how the largest of them, A & A, near Boston, operates.

A & A's main business is supplying retail bookstores, but it is glad to serve any library which is prepared to buy the way retailers buy: either in fairly substantial quantities, or at least with no more paper work than is tolerated by the Superintendent of Documents.

By and large, A & A's bookstore customers order by marking A & A's own catalogs and lists, where the publisher's title number appears beside the title. This accomplishes two things. In the first place, it prevents ordering titles that A & A doesn't stock. In the second place, it saves A & A a look-up to find the title number by which it does its picking, billing, and stock replenishing. The best guarantee of a happy relationship between A & A and any library customer would be a willingness on the part of the library to order the same way—from the A & A catalogs and lists, either sending in the marked lists themselves, or at least giving the publisher's title number.

Publishers' title numbers can usually also be picked up from the *PW* Weekly Record or *Paperbound Books in Print* or *Books in Print*, for example, Viking C126, Lancer 74-526. (These are not ISBNs, though hopefully they will yet be integrated into the ISBN system. They are more like the series numbers long used to identify the individual volumes in such series as Everyman's, Modern Library, or World's Classics.)

Ordering by title number isn't just a question of *who* does the look-up, you or A & A. If that were the only issue, A & A could just take the work off your shoulders and build the extra cost into its discount structure. Use of the number also means less chance of error and less chance of false reporting. Quite often libraries inadvertently order the paperback edition by the hardbound title, presumably because the latter was the title originally written on their order slip before they found the hardbound book was no longer available. When the number of the paperback title is given, trouble is averted. Otherwise, everybody's time may be wasted on the true but misleading report that there is no paperback by that title.

The greatest time-saver of all, for everybody, is making an effort not to ask A & A for the titles of publishers it doesn't stock. A & A tries to stock the paperback lines of some 300 publishers. It does not stock and does not special-order the paperback titles of the other 600 publishers who have titles listed in *Paperbound Books in Print.*

Unlike most hardbound wholesalers, A & A works with the publishers on an all-or-nothing basis. It tries to stock all the paperbacks of a given publisher, or none. (I think the major hardbound wholesalers would be doing themselves a real favor if they would move toward such a policy, under which they could say, "As a matter of policy we regularly stock *all* the titles of the following publishers." Then when you were in a hurry for a title, you wouldn't have to ask yourself, "Will my wholesaler have it, or had I better send direct to the publisher just to be sure?") A & A doesn't always succeed in getting a publisher's full line, as, for example, when the same publisher has both trade paperbacks and short-discount textbook paperbacks, but there is a sufficiently clean break between the lines it stocks and the lines it doesn't stock to make it worth your while to mark the distinction. Sending to A & A for an imprint it doesn't stock, and which you could have known in advance it did not stock, is a waste of everybody's time.

Once at a conference I found myself offering the foregoing advice to a school purchasing agent. He was quite indignant. He said, in effect, "Look, no vendor tells *me* how we'll do business. I tell him." Of course, that isn't quite true. He doesn't tell IBM how he'll write the computer rental contract; IBM tells him. He doesn't tell the phone company how they'll do business together; the phone company tells him. He doesn't tell the Library of Congress how he'll order its catalog cards; LC tells him.

Furthermore, telling the vendor how to do business isn't very wise. There are, unfortunately, too many purchasing agents whose power goes to their heads. Every salesman can tell you of many who think rudeness is toughness, who think chiseling is bargaining, and who wind up being wined, dined, flattered, and conned by vendors who fight fire with fire.

There is an old saying that you can't beat a man at his own game. And a chiseling purchasing agent can't beat a chiseling vendor. The only safety is in choosing vendors as carefully as employees, and changing them no less thoughtfully. I would guess that the purchasing agent quoted above by now gets few responses when he invites bids—and those only from fly-by-nights.

I think if I were trying to buy paperbacks for a library, I would try to follow these rules:

1.   Locate the nearest conscientious paperback retailer or college store, and plan to make buying visits on a regular schedule. Send someone authorized to select as well as just to buy from a list. Don't haggle over discount. You are trying to buy books, not discounts. Discuss with this bookseller the problem of how best to order the kind of title he doesn't stock. Get the names of the wholesalers he uses.

2.   Approach the wholesalers the bookseller recommends about helping you where he leaves off. Describe your needs in some detail. They'll be interested in knowing approximately how many books you expect to order over the course of a year, how many titles will make up a typical order, how often (if ever) you'll be asking them to fill single-copy orders, whether you'll pay promptly on their standard invoice without red tape, whether you'll expect them to back-order or cancel shorts, etc. Indicate an awareness of their problems by asking how they'd most prefer to have you order.

3.   Write direct to the publishers for your other needs. On single-copy orders enclose payment, at list price plus any handling charge the publisher may require. (He may state this in his other books.) If sending checks in advance "just isn't done" around your shop, get the rules changed in the interest of getting the books you need. Either that or write a personal check and then draw on petty cash or something to reimburse yourself.

4.   If your paperback needs are mixed — some singles, some quantities — it could pay you to buy everything through one wholesaler, even if you could get a bit more discount on the quantity lots by going direct to the publisher. You aren't going to find anyone interested in having you send him just your cats and dogs unless he gets a bit of the cream also.

5.   Negotiate your contracts; don't let them on bid. If you must let bids — well, *must* you? You could always quit and go to work for a library that doesn't require bids; the majority don't these days. Either that or change the basis of the bids so that *you* set the discount (about 10 percent higher than the last low bid), and award the business to the vendor who can fill the highest percentage of a large test order within two weeks. In other words, get the bidding basis shifted from discount to service.

Library Book Acquisitions—
The Publisher's Point of View

In a way everything in this book is from one publisher's point of view, namely mine, tempered by my years as publisher of the *Library Journal* and trustee of the Montclair Public Library.

Once I thought I'd be a physicist, but I found I liked what I saw of my father's way of life as editor of *Publishers' Weekly* (because he obviously liked it) and decided to go in that direction. His advice was: "In your first ten years out of college, don't concentrate, experiment. Move around. Try selling, editing, publicity, manufacturing, bookselling, book wholesaling, mail order. And look beyond the trade book field for the reasons why they do many things differently in the textbook, encyclopedia, technical, medical, educational, or children's book areas. If you do this methodically for ten years, you'll probably be ready to take your pick of some top jobs in your early thirties."

I followed that advice. In my first year out of college I was a sort of apprentice-learner with George Allen & Unwin of London, where I had an unparalleled opportunity to see a major publishing house from the inside; Sir Stanley Unwin would collect each day a carbon copy of each letter written anywhere in the company, and he let me study them. That year I also tried my hand at news reporting for the London *Bookseller* and before returning home spent time with three important book wholesalers, namely, W. H. Smith and Simpkin Marshall of London and Koehler & Volckmar of Leipzig.

Back in America I worked briefly for the University of Chicago Press, then did selling, manuscript reading, and publicity for Henry

Holt & Company; trade promotion, mail order, and advertising for the Oxford University Press of New York; office managing and manufacturing for the Alliance Book Corporation, then library promotion under May Massee in the children's book department of the Viking Press. I also worked one summer in the offices of the National Association of Book Publishers, doing research on a "code" for the publishing industry under the short-lived National Recovery Administration (NRA).

During World War II I was in Washington as director of the Treasury's war-bond program in the schools. In 1946 I was Director of the National Committee on Atomic Information, an effort of the atomic scientists to mobilize public opinion to head off the atomic arms race.

In 1947 I joined the R. R. Bowker Company. My first assignment was to try and get *Library Journal* out of the red, and my second assignment was to try to find a practical formula for indexing the *Publishers' Trade List Annual*, i.e., for producing a *Books in Print*. I never did get the time I had promised myself working in a bookstore, except for working nights in the Doubleday Fifth Avenue store for a number of weeks, and the closest I got to library work was putting my wife through Pratt Library School. She worked first under Anne Carroll Moore at several of the New York Public Library branches, later for the District of Columbia Public Library in the Jefferson Junior High School branch.

All told, I have had about 30 years in publishing (not counting the wartime digression). I ought to have acquired some opinions about library book acquisition problems from the publishers' point of view. And I have.

It is rash to generalize. Some publishers know very well indeed how important libraries are to them, in which group I would certainly include Fred Ruffner of Gale Research and Henry Z. Walck. In general, though, you can find within a single large house a welter of conflicting concepts and consequently varying policies on how best to serve libraries. Frequently there will be a well-informed library promotion director, but all contacts with the library wholesalers will be in another department.

In one large publishing house it was decided that it was uneconomic to keep in the catalog any title selling under 500 copies a year. At the very moment when such titles were being identified and remaindered, however, another department was being set up to make reprints of exactly the same kind of slow-selling title and was out actively seeking the very same kind of material. Let not the left hand know what the right hand doeth.

The sales manager of another large publishing house, suddenly conscious of the potential in the library market after the first of the big federal book appropriations, was told by a salesman that some libraries wouldn't buy direct because they wanted their books "processed." The sales manager demanded to know what "processed" meant. "Well," he was told, "you know how in libraries they have those numbers on the spines of the books? Well, they want those numbers."

An order immediately went out to the manufacturing department, "Put those library numbers on the spines of all our juveniles from now on." The manufacturing department replied, "No problem, but where do we get the numbers?" The answer was: "Off the copyright page, of course. You know where it says 'LC Card Number 00-00000.' Put that number!"

Fairly recently the treasurer of one of the major publishing houses, an old-timer, revealed to me in conversation that in trying to estimate the dimensions of his sales to libraries, he made the assumption that his sales to Baker & Taylor were predominantly going into bookstores rather than libraries. Of course, this hasn't been true since the 1920s. He probably would have made the same assumption about A. C. McClurg at the very time that an officer of that company was testifying in court that McClurg's book sales were 95 percent to schools and libraries.

It wasn't too many years ago that a former sales manager of Random House, by way of explaining why he opposed advertising in *Library Journal*, told me that he was certain that libraries were only a negligible factor in his sales of children's books. Of course, when he changed his mind, he did it in a big way and put out one of the industry's most active library sales forces.

Even today some publishers probably underestimate their own dependence on library purchasing. They are probably more aware than formerly that the library market is a big one (the best estimates I've been able to put together suggest that in 1968 libraries of all kinds probably spent about $250,000,000 for books), but they still tend to think as if the orders brought in by their salesmen were all going to bookstores, even though a moment's reflection would remind them that bookstores now account for a very small percentage indeed of the books sold to and by Baker & Taylor, Richard Abel, Bro-Dart, Campbell and Hall, etc. Today even a goodly portion of the books they sell to Bookazine and Dimondstein are going to libraries rather than bookstores.

A publisher gets precious little enlightenment from his trade salesmen about this. They aren't about to come back and say, "I am not sure I earn my 12 percent commission when I call on so-and-so. He only orders what the libraries order from him, and he'd have to do it whether I called or not."

Nor is the salesman necessarily insincere in this. In the sales interview, as mentioned earlier, he may be told by the wholesaler's buyer, "Well, we could probably move 100 instead of just 50 of this title, but why should we unless you give us some kind of incentive? Tell you what, we'll take 100 if you'll slip in an extra ten copies without charge for me to give my salesmen."

That certainly sounds as if some "selling" were going on, as distinct from just order taking, doesn't it? The salesman wouldn't be human if he didn't come away from such a sales interview feeling, "I earned my pay today. Because of my call, that library wholesaler took 100 instead of only 50."

A librarian, of course, might react somewhat differently, and say: "Now wait a minute. *I* decide what I buy, and I make my decisions on the merits of the books, not in response to any salesman's silver-tongued oratory. The wholesaler doesn't sway me, nor does he attempt to. Where does his buyer get off intimating to any publisher's representative that he has the power to sway my book selection decisions?"

This is an interesting point. *Is* there a role for the salesman in the library selection and acquisition process? Has he a contribution to make?

Let's concede that the cited sales interview was mostly bluff. Wholesalers have only the tiniest of sales forces by comparison to publishers; they often handle their entire operation—ordering, shelving, picking, billing, shipping, collecting, rent, taxes, and salaries—on a part of the libraries' book dollar not much larger than some publishers pay in commission to their salesmen.

The bluff works because the people who make the sales decisions in publishing offices usually started as salesmen to bookstores. In their minds they imagine the wholesaler selling to libraries the way *they* sold to bookstores. They imagine the salesman going in and saying: "Now *this* is going to be dynamite, take my word for it, take 100. The author's last one tickled the critics where they live; this one is going to tickle the readers, believe me. Prepare for it. Full return privileges, of course."

The pub rep must believe—for his own self-respect—that *his* presence on the scene can increase sales. He is therefore ready to believe that it must be the same with any salesmen the wholesaler employs.

85

But *do* salesmen really increase sales for their employers — at least enough to earn their commissions, which typically run to 10 or 12 percent of the invoiced total and may run to 20? (In some situations, the salesman gets more than the author.)

If you detect on my part a certain skepticism about this, your antennae are in good working order. If I were a librarian, I don't believe I'd *see* publishers' sales representatives. Granted, they break the monotony, they bring the latest gossip, they stand treat on nice lunches, they are good company. But they could be adding as much as 10 percent to the cost of the books you buy, and their job is to get not merely their fair share of your book-buying dollar, but more than their share.

I once asked a publisher how he could possibly justify a 20-percent commission to the salesmen he had calling on libraries. My reasoning was that there was a lot of business in any territory that he was bound to get anyway, whether he sent in a salesman or not. It followed that even if the salesman were able to double the business, a 20-percent commission on all of it would be like a 40-percent commission on the increase. Of course, salesmen's commissions are figured on the net, not the list, and 40 percent of the net may be only about 26 percent of list. Still . . .

The publisher only said: "Well, we *are* more than doubling our share of the business. Why, sometimes the right man in the right place at the right time can get *all* of a superintendent's federal book money for our line alone."

That was several years ago. The next year, as I heard it, things were a little tougher. A call on the same superintendent might produce only the comment that "we bought your books *last* year."

Actually, most publishers would probably prefer *not* to employ a sales force to call on schools and libraries; their reasons for doing it are mainly defensive. They know that their most aggressive competitor is out to increase his share of the market at their expense, and they figure that unless they get in there and fight fire with fire, they will wind up with less than their share of the market. One librarian who prefers not to be quoted by name writes:

> As librarians, we need to develop more skill in saying "No" to publishers' salesmen. In our dealings with the public all our energies are properly devoted to saying "Yes." An interview is a failure unless the other fellow goes away happy. We aim to please.
> We cannot, however, "aim to please" a publisher's salesman in anything like the same sense. What a salesman wants is *more than his proper share of our book money*, and

we can't say "Yes" to that and still do right by our patrons, our professional standards, and those other publishers and authors whose share would be less if the man in our office succeeds in getting more.

The reason why publishers' direct-to-library sales forces have proliferated is simply because they have found that we are easy marks. Putting a man in my office to sell me books costs, I have heard, perhaps $160 or so a day, and how many calls can a man complete in one day? If his interview with me costs his employer (in salary, travel, and other expenses) $50, what result does he consider satisfactory? Obviously it is money down the drain if I buy only those books I would have bought without the visit. Clearly I must buy at least $250 worth of books I would not otherwise have bought if the cost of the salesman's visit is to be held under 20 percent of the publishers' receipts.

Some of the most successful department store buyers have a reputation among the salesmen of being flinty-eyed skeptics who get their kicks out of saying "No." Maybe they know something we must learn, namely, that any desire to please the salesman *must be excluded* from any buying decision. Be a nice guy everywhere else, but in the sales interview make 'em hate your guts.

I know the arguments in favor of using salesmen. After all, I used to be one. The argument is that salesmen don't really add anything to the cost of doing business, because they increase sales and this decreases costs. Publishers may make only a modest profit on the *average* book sale, but they make a much larger one on each *added* sale. A printing of 5,000 copies may cost $5,000, or $1 a copy, but a printing of 6,000 copies may cost only $5,500, with the extra 1,000 copies costing only an extra 50 cents apiece. If an extra salesman can help sell the extra 1,000 books, his commission can come out of such cost savings.

I sometimes respond to this argument by noting that as regards libraries, the combined total of their book-buying money does not increase merely because some of the publishers put salesmen into the field. The effect of the salesmen cannot be to increase overall book sales; it can only be to switch some of the expenditures from one set of publishers to others. The publisher with the sales force doesn't reduce his prices as sales rise; he has to pay the difference to the salesmen. And the publisher without the sales force must raise his prices as sales fall. So book prices do go up as a result of adding a payment to library sales forces.

I am sometimes told, of course, that a sales force can increase the amount of money being spent on books. It can go get money for books that might not otherwise have been spent on books at all. There is

87

lots of money that might go for language labs, or intercoms, or something else if the book salesmen weren't in there fighting.

Well, I don't know. I never saw a salesman out beating the bushes for marginal business. Salesmen know how to put first things first. They don't go scrabbling in the boondocks until after they have first picked all the plums that are ripe for the picking right in the buying offices of the big libraries in their territory.

Once upon a time I thought I had a bright idea about increasing the sale of *Books in Print*. People who bought it once usually went on buying it every year, but I had never tried any sales approach other than advertising and direct mail. I worked up a deal with the head of one of the largest library sales forces for his men to sell it. You know what happened? They reported that all the libraries they called on already had it. And that meant they were calling on less than 4,000 libraries at the time, whereas by direct mail the library sale eventually went up past 20,000.

So I would say again: In the library field, which is what we are talking about, salesmen don't increase sales, at best they switch sales, and mostly they just take credit for sales that were there all along. I'm not for outlawing salesmen. I think they have an important role to play in calling on bookstores. I'm not sure it's enough, though, just to sit with the buyer and run through the fall catalog. A salesman ought to help check the stock on the shelves, and ought to spot missing staples and perhaps suggest the return of dead stock and its replacement with titles of greater potential. It wouldn't hurt if he carried a supply of replacement jackets to use in freshening up dog-eared stock.

Frankly, I'd like to see most of the salesmen taken off the road, brought into the office, and set to following through on complaints. Complaints about publishers' service are legion, and one can only hope that the worst sinners take some punishment from libraries with a policy of canceling long-overdue orders and spending the money elsewhere.

Much of the comment at and following the ALA Pre-Conference on Acquisitions in 1969 was a plea for more intelligent action by publishers on library needs. Some of the most frequently reiterated comments were:

> I don't want to buy direct from the publisher, I don't want to see his salesmen. But I can't help myself if he undersells his own wholesaler outlets. This ought to be against the law.

I think I've found a wholesaler who knows how to serve me the way I want to be served. If anyone thinks that 100 different publishers could ever all learn to serve me as well, he's dreaming. Publishers should publish; wholesalers should distribute.

As long as I can remember we have all been pleading with the publishers to get together on a uniform reporting system, so we could tell where we stood on back-ordered items. I can't see that they have ever taken Step One. Some heads need to be knocked together on this.

Where publishers go wrong is in underestimating the variety and complexity of the library market. We aren't all going to want the same thing, ever. Schools are not public libraries, and public libraries are not research libraries. Some of us are large, some are small. Some of us want the new books at least as early as the bookstores get them; some don't push for this. Some of us prefer to put all our orders through a wholesaler; others order direct whenever we think it might save some time, or whenever we want to double-check a report from our wholesaler that the book is unobtainable. There is no *one way* to do business with libraries or anyone else, unless perhaps it is to do business the way each customer wants it done.

Publishers solicit our direct orders, then complain about the paper work that our business office insists on. But our wholesaler doesn't complain because our orders to him are big enough to justify it. So why don't the publishers stop soliciting our direct orders and make a place for our wholesaler in their scheme of distribution?

With or without sending his own salesmen to make direct calls on libraries, each publisher must work out the terms on which he will let the wholesalers compete with him. Where trade books are concerned, the policy of many publishers was (and in many cases still is) to let the discounts to wholesalers rise to 46 percent or so, so that the wholesaler could readily resell to libraries at 30 percent off or better, while the publisher himself filled direct library orders at 25 off. Under these conditions, the bulk of the library business went through wholesalers.

The bigger libraries, however, began to play off the wholesalers against each other for bigger discounts: 35 percent, 36, 37, 38, even 40 and 41. It got so that even libraries of moderate size could get 36 or so, provided their needs were not unusually complex.

It now became a matter of survival for the wholesaler to handle only those books on which his markup covered his costs. If he couldn't get his books at 46 off, he couldn't afford to fulfill his contracts. Sometimes he could cumulate orders and anticipate needs so as to build up a quantity order to the point where he'd get his 46 or better. When he couldn't, as in the case of some of the smaller publishers, he'd often prefer not to handle that publisher's books at all rather than to handle them at a loss.

As mentioned elsewhere, it soon got so some wholesalers would just sit back and not supply the less profitable items, even though their library customers had every reason to expect them to do so under their contract. They'd report the titles as out of stock, leaving the impression that of course they were on order, and hopefully the library would eventually tire of waiting and cancel.

A question you must ask yourself is whether your wholesaler is steering you, subtly or otherwise, away from the titles of publishers he'd prefer not to handle or whom he wants to punish for not giving him more operating margin. I am not suggesting that a wholesaler should be forced to handle any line he doesn't want to handle; he must, however, tell you he doesn't. Fair enough if he tells you frankly, "We can't afford to handle this line on the margin the publisher gives us; please order direct from the publisher." It is neither fair nor honest, however, to give you the impression that a title you have ordered is out of stock, when in fact it is completely available from the publisher and even from other wholesalers.

Perhaps it could be argued that a library ought to *support* its supplier in his efforts to get more discount out of the publishers, since the more discount he gets, the more he can pass along. This could be well and good, provided you know what he's doing and approve it. There are two big dangers. First, the supplier may *not* pass on to you any extra money he gets out of the publishers, especially if you don't know he's getting it; and second, any general increase in his discounts and your discounts will simply lead the publisher to increase his list prices.

The pricing and discounting of books are full of complexities and misunderstandings. Some may be worth exploring here.

The wholesaler who looks at his year-end profit and wishes it were higher is, of course, squeezed between what he can charge you and what the publishers or his employees get from him. He is bound to think longingly about how wonderful it would be if he could just get another 1 percent of discount from the publishers. At the very least, he will brood about how the best discount he gets from any publisher should be matched by all the others. Of course, he knows, whether he admits it to himself or not, that more discount isn't the answer to his problems and never will be, since if he got more discount, so would his competitors, and if everybody got more discount, the bidding for your contract would reflect it, and he'd get less from you and be right back where he started.

He must be sure, of course, that the discounts he is getting are not *inferior* to those his competitors are getting. Any such discrimination by the publishers between wholesalers would be illegal under the Robinson-Patman Act, but he is bound to worry about this and very likely seek reassurance by pressing hard for more discount, just to see whether any of the publishers might yield.

He knows, too (whether he admits it to himself or not), that discount isn't everything. What really counts most is gross margin *per unit transaction*. A line of higher-priced books, such as technical books, might give him more dollars of profit even at less percent. Alternately, a low-priced line commonly sold in twos, fives, or tens of a title might give him more profit than a higher-priced line usually sold in ones.

Fundamentally the wholesaler can exert only the most limited control over what he pays the publishers. Does it follow, then, that there is no way that librarians or wholesalers can make their displeasure felt, and effective, where they believe publishers are overcharging? The most potent weapon open to librarians is the simple refusal to buy. Another weapon is a policy of "buying around" (from England) where the opportunity exists and the provocation seems flagrant.

I have heard some librarians say—off the record—that price is irrelevant to their buying decisions. Either they want a book or they don't. If they want it, an extra few dollars won't stop them, and if they don't want it enough to pay its price, then they probably wouldn't want it even as a gift, considering the cost of processing and housing.

I have heard other librarians say: "It must be nice to have that kind of book budget. Our librarians are quite price-conscious. To be sure, they'd probably pay whatever it costs rather than go without Milne or Kipling, but many a good but high-priced book has been considered and then dropped from an order list in favor of two equally good but lower-priced books. And increasingly the assigned summer reading lists are *limited* to books available in low-priced editions."

The biggest bone of contention between wholesalers and publishers is competition between the two for the libraries' business. Several publishers, including Random House, Doubleday, Prentice-Hall, and Macmillan, have large sales forces actively seeking to go around the wholesalers to their best library customers. In such a competition, clearly the publisher can win on discount if he chooses, since he controls everything: list price, the discount he gives the wholesaler, and the discount he gives the library. There is no way in which the wholesaler can win this competition if the publisher wants it otherwise. Under the Robinson-Patman Act, a publisher must treat two competing wholesalers alike, so that any competition between them for the business of the same library is on an even footing. But the Robinson-Patman Act simply does not apply in the area of competition between publishers and wholesalers. The publisher is entirely free to undersell his own wholesale outlets.

For a few years this competition was under wraps, thanks to a sort of unwritten agreement that the publishers would not undercut the wholesalers if the wholesalers would not undercut the publishers. The idea was that a publisher's salesman might call on a library only to lose the resulting order to the library's regular wholesaler, but the decision was the librarian's, and it could be made on the basis of convenience and service, not discount. In my opinion, this might have worked fairly well if the wholesalers' margin had been limited to about 25 percent of the library net price, but some of the publishers let themselves be pressured into giving 33⅓ percent, and others followed. It was a foolish move.

To review the story of what happened, you will remember that in the days before publishers fully sensed the growth potential in school libraries, these libraries channeled much of their book buying through E. M. Hale or prebinders like H. R. Huntting and New Method Book Bindery to get bindings which would stand the wear and tear of repeated circulations—something the publisher's trade binding usually would not do, designed as it was with the idea that the book would be bought by one reader and read once.

The bindings on the inexpensive Golden Books were among the most vulnerable, and Golden moved to correct this deficiency by making books with library potential available in "Goldencraft" editions with washable cloth covers and strong sewing instead of glue. They offered excellent durability for the price. While these bindings were not as strong as the Class A binding specifications adhered to by the prebinders, neither were they as expensive.

(It is worth noting, by the way, that the Class A specifications for library binding are not an ALA or government standard, but were drawn up by the Library Binding Institute, a trade association representing the binders who specialized in serving libraries. With few if any exceptions, only members of the LBI have the special "oversewing" machinery required to be used under the Class A specifications. Believing that the Class A binding was needlessly strong and expensive except where hundreds of circulations were expected, an ALA committee introduced the so-called LUMSPECS, or Lesser Used Materials Specifications.)

The Goldencraft bindings posed a new pricing problem. There was no expectation of any sale in bookstores, so there was little point in setting a "retail price" that no one would pay. The editions were to be sold direct by a special Goldencraft library sales force, but it was recognized that many libraries would prefer to order them through their regular wholesaler, or perhaps their regular prebinder. The question was: How could these books be priced and discounted to allow a fair profit margin for the wholesalers and prebinders and yet not tempt them to undersell the Goldencraft salesmen? It seemed fairest to strive for a pricing policy under which the price paid by the libraries would be the same no matter where they bought, so that they would not be forced to buy from a low-service supplier merely because he had shaved the price a little.

After some study of the margins needed by wholesalers, it was decided to give them a discount of 25 percent from the net prices at which the Goldencraft salesmen would sell, and hope that the wholesalers, too, would sell at these prices. It was recognized that many of the wholesalers were operating on margins of 16 percent or less (i.e., 16 percent of their selling price, as would be the case, for example, if they were buying at 46 percent off list and selling at 36 percent off list), but it was recognized also that other, higher-service wholesalers and booksellers seemed to need 25 percent — which would be their effective margin if they were buying at 40 off and selling at 20 off.

Clearly a margin of 25 percent on these highly salable books was more than most wholesalers seemed to need, but Goldencraft preferred to lean over backward not to take advantage of its power to squeeze the wholesalers out of the picture.

The wholesalers were delighted and initially took as much care not to undersell the Goldencraft men as the latter were obviously taking not to undersell the wholesalers. This seemed only prudent, since it was clear that Goldencraft was bound to win if it came to a price war.

Business boomed. Other publishers began offering library bindings. The big wholesalers began to order in huge quantities and in short order had wheedled quantity discounts running up to 33⅓ percent. It was a foolish move, born of naiveté on the part of the publishers' sales managers, one of whom once said to me in wide-eyed innocence, "But what was wrong with 33⅓ percent? My gosh, we used to give them 46 percent."

What was wrong was that at 46 percent the wholesaler would commonly buy a $5 book at $2.70 and sell it to the library at $3.25 for an operating ma .jin of 55 cents. Now he was invited to buy (say) a $4.50 book at $3.00 and sell it to the library at $4.50. This gave him an operating margin of $1.50 as against the former 55 cents, and of course he was transported with joy. But so were his competitors, and there was no more chance of keeping those fabulous extra-profit margins under cover than of containing the steam in a kettle by clamping on the lid. The big libraries found themselves wooed so ardently that they could *smell* the profit margin, and they dug in their heels and insisted on having some of it. After all, they had traditionally gotten more discount than smaller libraries; why not now? They were offered almost any terms they cared to name on the other books they needed by any wholesaler whom they would favor with their orders for these super-profitable "net-priced" editions.

Too late, the publishers waked up to what their sales forces had been getting them into, to find the Justice Department investigating charges that they had conspired to defraud the government by fixing prices, and to face later suits by the Philadelphia Public Library and others to recover the alleged overcharges.

It was a curious case, inasmuch as the publishers appeared to have acted more to preserve competition (on service) than to eliminate it, had not themselves profited, had usually offered the net-priced edition in addition to the regular trade edition, so the library could still buy the other if it preferred, and had remained throughout in hot competition *with each other*. (*Real* price-fixing would probably have taken the form of some such agreement as not to offer any Grimm's Fairy Tales under $4, and of course no such thing happened.)

The Justice Department concluded there was no conspiracy, and said in effect, "It may not have been dishonest, boys, but it wasn't very smart, so just don't do it again."

An outcry went up, however, that libraries *had* been overcharged, inasmuch as the wholesalers were now freely giving discounts on editions they had been selling only at net prices, and that it ought to be possible to sue someone and collect triple damages. Various libraries were persuaded to try it, very likely by lawyers willing to take a chance on getting paid out of any winnings.

Estimating damages had its problems, because in general the libraries had been getting more discount than normal on the other books they bought, to make up for the fact that they were getting less on the net-priced editions. The worst that could be charged was that first one publisher and then another, each for reasons sufficient unto himself, had tried (if ineptly) to arrive at a live-and-let-live philosophy for putting a sales force into the field without depriving libraries of the privilege of ordering through wholesalers. And it might have worked if the discount to the wholesalers had been set at *about what they needed* instead of a lot higher.

Now that the publishers have been spanked, the earlier problem rears its head again. Both publishers and wholesalers want that lush big-library business. Shall the publisher go after it by increasing the discounts he offers to libraries or by decreasing what the wholesaler can offer by giving him less discount? By either route the wholesaler sees the publisher trying to take the cream of the library business and leave him the skim milk.

Some perspective on this struggle can perhaps be drawn from history. Once all books moved through bookstores. Then the publishers went around them on elementary and high school textbooks, encyclopedias, and via bookclubs and newsstands. Once bookstores were the chief suppliers of libraries. Then the wholesalers went around them. The publishers were astonishingly slow to sense the size of the library market, but now they are going around the wholesalers.

Will the wholesalers be pushed out of the picture? It seems unlikely. Despite the bookstore's loss of one specialized market after another, bookstores are still with us, and if you expand the "bookstore" concept to embrace all retail book outlets, book retailing is bigger than ever.

To my mind, what is coming is a transitional period during which libraries are going to find it difficult not to order from those publishers who are outbidding the wholesalers, but during which both parties are going to learn that wholesaling has its place.

To be sure, wholesaling to bookstores has been almost killed by the direct-selling policies of the publishers and survives in only limited areas. Libraries, however, are not quite as easy to serve as bookstores; their wants are more complex.

Every publisher who has put out a sales force has promptly been told by his salesmen that "we're dead if we don't give catalog cards, or processing kits, or preprocessing, or approval plan services," etc. It is conceivable that a few — a very few — big publishers might eventually learn to provide such services as efficiently as the best wholesalers are learning to provide them, but certainly the great majority of publishers will never do it. Already the publishers' efforts to provide standing-order services are producing wide dissatisfaction. And how, pray tell, could it be otherwise? How could scores and hundreds of publishers each ever know enough about the special needs of thousands of libraries to give them this kind of highly personalized service? This is surely a job for a wholesaler.

A library's buying policies inevitably have to accommodate themselves to some degree to the publishers' selling policies. Some publishers sell only direct, giving no discounts whatever to anyone and perhaps refusing to sell to wholesalers even at full list price unless the wholesaler supplies the name of the library for which he is acting.

Some publishers *prefer* to sell direct, but attempt to provide a practical alternative to those libraries which prefer to place all their orders through a wholesaler. Such publishers try to allow the wholesaler enough discount to operate on, but not so much that he will be able to undercut the publisher's price.

Some publishers expect to do very little direct selling and build their pricing and discount structure around the expectation of selling primarily through wholesalers and retailers.

The pricing structure of primary interest to libraries is, of course, the so-called "trade-book" pricing structure. Other segments of the book-publishing industry, notably elementary and high school textbooks, college textbooks, encyclopedias, and scientific, technical, and medical books, may be bigger than trade books in total dollar sales but are a smaller factor in the library book-buying picture.

Each structure must be understood and provided for, of course, since most libraries sooner or later find themselves needing something even from publishers who are not accustomed to sell to libraries. However, trade books are the first category dealt with in almost all library book contract negotiations. Trade books are so called because they are priced and discounted to enable them to be distributed through the book trade, i.e., the booksellers.

At one time wholesalers bought from the publishers at list price less 46 percent, booksellers bought from the wholesalers or publishers at list price less 40 percent, and libraries bought from the booksellers at whatever discount they could get, commonly 20 or 25 percent. Then the wholesalers began to take the library business away from the retailers by outbidding them, which they could easily do, since they were getting more discount themselves. Much more recently, some of the publishers began to take library business away from the wholesalers, and, of course, were able to outbid them at will since they controlled the whole pricing picture.

Wholesalers no longer get more discount than retailers merely because they are wholesalers. Under the Robinson-Patman Act, a publisher must not give better discounts to a wholesaler than he gives to a retailer if both are bidding on the same library contract, except as he can justify the difference on the basis of volume. He can give larger discounts to the wholesaler only if the wholesaler orders in larger quantities. The usual scale is as shown on page 66.

Having set out the schedule of discounts under which he will supply wholesalers and retailers, the publisher must also decide whether he wishes to sell around them, to their customers, i.e., to the libraries and the general public. Many publishers set their library discounts at 25 percent off list, i.e., well below the discounts they know the wholesalers are offering. In effect, they are saying: "We will accept direct business from the libraries, but we will not encourage it. We'd rather sell to the trade at higher discounts instead of to the libraries at lower discounts, because the trade buys in a businesslike way and pays promptly, whereas too many libraries want to be billed on their forms instead of ours and take an inordinate time to pay."

The Economics of Book Pricing

Some background on how books are priced will perhaps be of help to you in evaluating discounts. If someone offers you books at 60 percent off list, or something equally wild, look for the reason. There is no Santa Claus. Nobody, but nobody, can buy the regular run of regular trade books at much better than 46 percent off list, and anyone who says he can should explain how.

Original editions offered at deep cuts from original prices could be remainders, or they could be premiums to get you to join some kind of book club. Remainders and premiums can be real bargains, though the title selection isn't likely to be very wide. You need to be on your guard, though. Some bargain package deals are like boxes of strawberries, the only good berries being the ones on top.

How does a publisher arrive at a price for a book? An old rule in publishing says, "Set your list price at five times your manufacturing cost." This rule is good economics but poor public relations. It makes the publisher seem like a profiteer when, in fact, any publisher who follows this rule (and most trade publishers do to some extent) will nevertheless end by paying out to his printers and his authors well over half of everything he takes in from the book wholesalers and retail booksellers.

The old conundrum asks, "Which came first, the hen or the egg?" It has its parallel in the question, "Do publishers first decide on a list price and then work back to what they can afford to spend on manufacture, or do they let the manufacturing cost determine the list price?" Usually the only possible answer is, "It depends. . . ."

97

Sometimes a publisher will ask himself a series of questions like the following: "Would readers consider $10 a reasonable price for this book?" "If we published at $10, how many do we think we could sell?" "If we printed that many, what would they cost per copy?"

If this last figure, the tentative cost, is less than one-fifth of the first figure, the tentative $10 list price, the publisher breathes a sigh of relief and assumes that the other cost factors will work out, because the other cost factors tend to be proportional to the list price. On a typical $10 trade book his other costs might work out about as follows:

	Income	Outgo
Net receipts (figured at list price less 44%)	$5.60	
Manufacturing cost		$2.00
Author's royalty (figured at 12½% of list price)		1.25
Advertising (figured at 10% of list price)		1.00
Salesmen's salary or commissions (figured at 10% of net receipts)		.56
Warehousing, shipping, billing (figured at 8% of net receipts)		.45
Other overheads (managers, editors, bookkeepers, rent, utilities, etc.)		.75
Total costs before profit and taxes		6.01
Total revenue	5.60	

There would appear to be something dreadfully wrong with this calculation, since on the face of it the publisher loses money on every copy. Unfortunately that is precisely what happens on the typical original edition of a new book, even if the first edition sells out. Where the publisher hopes to recoup, of course, is either through the sale of additional printings or through participation in the revenue from subsidiary rights, such as book-club rights, reprint rights, translation rights, serialization rights, motion-picture rights.

If the sale justifies a second printing, the cost per copy will be lower (the type is paid for) and usually the advertising costs will be lower. Part of the saving may go to the author in increased royalty, but in general a book that becomes a steady seller on the backlist becomes a profitable property for the publisher.

On many a book the publisher miscalculates and ends with a pile of unsold and unsalable copies. Then the next time he needs shelf space (or ready cash) he calls in a remainder dealer.

The remainder dealer goes through a pricing calculation very similar to the publisher's. He says to himself, "What do I think readers would pay for this $10 book as a remainder? $5.95? $4.95? $3.95? $1.98? $1.49?" Then he makes the publisher an offer of perhaps $1.50 for a title he thinks he could retail at $4.95 and perhaps 50 cents for a title he feels would bring only $1.49. (As a rule, the author gets no royalty on books that are remaindered.) The best remainder prices are paid for nonfiction, provided it isn't dated. Unsuccessful fiction often can't be sold at any price.

The books that get remaindered are not necessarily bad books. Some, in fact, were successes—the publisher simply went back to press for one reprint too many. Remainders are often extremely good buys, and the offerings of the remainder dealers are well worth watching.

Sometimes you'll see a book offered at a deeply cut remainder price that your wholesaler or the publisher just sold you at regular price. This is annoying, to say the least, but probably unavoidable. What happens is that the publisher finds himself with (say) 4,500 copies of a title that has simmered down to an annual rate of sale of about 100 copies a year. In other words, he has what looks like a 45-year supply. He keeps what he estimates to be a ten-year supply and sells off the other copies to a remainder house.

Publishers are sometimes criticized for this so-called "partial remaindering" on the grounds that anyone ordering the full-price edition while the remainder is still on the market ought to be warned. In general, I think publishers would agree, if as a practical matter this were possible. It really isn't possible, however. In the first place, the publisher usually doesn't know how the remainder will be priced, how long it will stay on sale, or where it will be sold. In the second place, not many buyers will be affected, since (at a rate of sale of 100 copies a year) the publisher may not get a dozen orders between the time the remainder goes on sale and the time it is sold out. Finally, the publisher can reason that he might get no thanks even from those he was trying to help if he were to write would-be buyers and say, "Before I fill your order I better warn you that you might be able to buy it cheaper from Marboro, though I am not dead sure how they are pricing it, and I can't tell you whether they would accept an order for a single copy, or even whether they still have any."

Perhaps you have wondered how it is possible for essentially the same book to sell at (say) $10 in cloth and $2.95 in a quality paper-bound edition. Sometimes there is little or no difference in the paper, or the size of type, or the margins—and certainly not $7 worth of difference in the binding.

One difference is that the cost of setting type and sending out review copies is usually charged against the original $10 edition, and all this has been paid for by the time the reprint comes along. Another big difference is in the amount paid to the author. An author may get $1.50 a copy on a $10 book (more than 25 percent of the publisher's net receipts). He may get only 10 cents or so on the $2.95 edition, where a common royalty is 7 percent of the $2.95 divided equally between original publisher and author.

When it comes to working out the economics of a mass-market edition priced at (say) 95 cents, first, the amount of paper involved is sharply reduced (smaller type, smaller page, smaller margins, thinner paper); second, the paper is of cheaper quality; and, finally, the royalty to author and original publisher is less.

Some say I oversimplify, but I personally get a lot of mileage out of the following rules of thumb: Setting type costs about 2 cents a word. Paper, printing, and binding cost about 55 cents a pound. That is to say, a typical two-pound book will cost about $1.10 for paper, printing, and binding, give or take 20 cents, unless the number printed is exceptionally small or the book is unusual in some other way.

Book Selection—How Publishers
Influence It, or Try to

Publishers work hard at trying to sway you in your book-selection decisions. They hire special library promotion people, compile and mail catalogs, advertise, send out review copies and publicity releases, exhibit at conventions, and even arrange for salesmen to call.

I did that kind of work for three publishers, and I did a lot of soul-searching about whether any of it was effective. Once I incautiously asked a librarian which influenced her more, advertising or direct mail. You'd have thought I'd asked whether her parents had ever married. She said indignantly, "I *never* permit myself to be influenced by commercial propaganda."

All right, then, what did she go by? The reviews? The bibliographic checklists? Personal inspection of the books? Word-of-mouth recommendations from friends?

It was my *job* to influence her, or at least to see that she got the information she needed for making her decisions. Frequently I would be the one to write the jacket blurb, write the catalog copy, write the publicity releases, write the advertising copy, set up and man the convention exhibit booth. Was I to believe that nothing I did mattered, unless perhaps I were to forget to send out advance copies to the key bibliographies and the review journals? (I *did* once completely forget to send out any review copies. The book was a British author's fourth mystery novel. It sold better without reviews than its predecessors had sold with reviews.)

I believe now that the most effective elements in book promotion are the least glamorous. The publisher's publicity person may have to arrange parties and publicity and interviews to please the author, but what *counts* is getting the book into *Forthcoming Books*, the *Lj* and *PW* announcement issues, Kirkus, *Choice*, the *Booklist*, the wholesalers' catalogs, etc. What *counts* is getting the earliest possible review copy into the hands of LC, so the LC cataloging can be ready early, and the listing in the *PW* Weekly Record will not be held up, and the book itself can go into library circulation on or near publication day.

Launching a book effectively is something like lighting a campfire with one match. Publication day is the match. You don't want to strike it until your tinder is ready (the advance reviews and quotes), the kindling is in place (the books are in the bookstores), and the firewood is at hand (the advertising).

Or you could liken the launching of a book to the setting off of an atomic chain reaction. You can't have an atomic chain reaction until you bring together a certain "critical mass" of fissionable materials. To give a new book a fighting chance of taking off, the reviews, the publicity, the bookstore display, and the advertising should all be coordinated and unleashed within a limited time span to interreact effectively.

The publishers' library promotion people are necessarily competitive in their promotion. They want you to buy their titles instead of somebody else's. They also want to have something to show for their efforts — to show the boss, or show the author. This leads to too many circulars and not enough cooperative selection aids. When an author wants to know what anybody is doing for his book, they'd rather be able to show him direct mail pieces, advertising, publicity releases, posters, etc., than just to show him how he got into the Combined Book Exhibit catalogs or the *PW* Weekly Record.

However, an author whose book gets all its proper listings in all the Bowker publications, all the Wilson publications, all the LC publications, all the ALA publications, all the wholesalers' catalogs and

101

checklists, Kirkus, and then perhaps the British counterparts of all these—that author can be shown that quite a lot of people are doing quite a lot to make his book known.

If you can find out about the book in any bookstore or library anywhere; if you can find out about it before publication, on publication, and after publication; if you can look it up by author, or by title, or by subject; and if you can find out years after it first came out the latest price and whether it is still in print—that's pretty remarkable when you think about it.

I was really taken aback by the lady who denied being influenced by my "commercial propaganda." I now believe she was wrong, though. She was influenced whether she knew it or not.

I am a firm believer in what I call the "three-nudge" theory of book promotion. The first time you see or hear the title of a new book you don't pay much attention. The second time it begins to sound familiar. The third time you think, "Say, I've been hearing a lot about that. . . ." The effect is the same whether the first two nudges were news items, reviews, displays, ads, or whatever.

If this is a fair picture of the way a new book creeps into *your* consciousness, don't fight it—welcome it. There is nothing wrong with letting yourself be influenced by the same forces that influence John Q. Reader. The more you can react as he does, the better you can serve him. I would only suggest that librarians have a special responsibility also to the author whose book failed (for whatever reason) to get that third nudge, the author who might be unjustly in danger of being overlooked.

Of course, an author still won't get much of a run for his message if nobody hears about him and nobody looks him up by author or by title. And it won't help as much as it should to have readers learn about his book when searching under subject only to find the library doesn't have it.

In this respect, libraries are of critical importance in preserving freedom of speech and press. Despite the tendencies toward mergers and bigness, there are still literally thousands of independent publishers. And a good many of them owe their very existence to those conscientious librarians who make it their business to find out about books whether or not they are advertised, and to buy them whether or not a salesman calls, and whether or not their wholesaler stocks them.

Cataloging—Means or End?

There has surely never been a catalog so carefully compiled and corrected that a new cataloger could not privately say, "What a mess," upon opening any drawer. For that matter, there has probably never been a Library of Congress catalog card that wouldn't have been done slightly differently if put through a month earlier while Mr. X was still around, or a month later while Miss Y was on vacation.

I had a dramatic demonstration of this while compiling the first edition of the *Subject Guide to Books in Print*. Our procedure had been to look up every title in the LC catalogs, copy off the subject headings LC had assigned, create a new entry card for each heading, and finally file the new cards by subject heading.

What a mess! Not only did we have to identify and change all the headings which LC itself had first assigned and later rejected and changed. (There was an evolution, as I recall, from Mechanical Data Processing to Electronic Data Processing to Data Processing, Automatic.) And not only did we have to make judgments about how many listings under a heading were too few to warrant retention of some of LC's sub-sub-subheadings. (We were, after all, dealing with only about 150,000 titles, whereas LC had been dealing with 50 times as many.) But we had to decide which *style* of LC subject cataloging we liked the best, because clearly there had been periods when LC's catalogers hadn't hesitated to assign five or more subject headings to a single book and other periods when three subject headings per title seemed to be the practical working limit. Under the direction of Herbert B. Anstaett, then librarian of Franklin and Marshall College, we put in thousands of hours adapting LC to the needs of *Subject Guide.*

I trust that I have never since then failed to be sympathetic when catalogers insist that you can't just "file" a set of LC cards, however "official" they may be. You have to make sure they fit. You don't want to enter a new title under "Data Processing, Automatic" without at least a cross-reference from any prior titles still filed under "Electronic Data Processing."

On the other hand, since no catalog can ever do more than *aspire* to perfection in this all-too-imperfect world, it does seem to me that we need more guidance on how to be imperfect. We need some hard-headed priorities to help us know when a book in the reader's hand is worth two in central processing.

Take, for example, the next 100 patrons who enter the library seeking (whether they know it or not) a book that has only just arrived but has not yet been processed. What is the single most useful thing we could have done to help them?

Most libraries have long since thought out their answer and acted on it—they have put a temporary author entry in the public catalog. Whether the patron comes in armed with author and title (perhaps from the same source that prompted the library to place its order) or whether he is led to this information after entering the library, perhaps through any of the standard reviewing media or current bibliographies, he can at least then learn swiftly and directly that the desired book has been ordered and may be in the house. He may not be able as yet to find the book by looking under title or under subject, but he either knows, or will be told if he seeks help, that the *first* place to look is under author.

Grant me, temporarily, the hypothesis that 40 of these 100 patrons might reasonably be expected to identify the book they need with no more help than a temporary author entry in the public catalog. (Of course, if you aren't going to let them have it once they know *you* have it, you may not want them to have this information.)

In my example, we have, however, left 60 of our 100 patrons unsatisfied. These are the ones who did not know author and title and may not even have suspected that such a book existed, though they would have been helped by it. Is there any practical way of helping these others to learn about the book, despite the fact that it has not yet been fully cataloged?

Again, most libraries have at least a strong hunch about this. If

Priority One involves putting a temporary author entry in the public catalog, Priority Two would involve getting the book onto the open shelves, in the appropriate section, if this were deemed practical. Where this can be done, using provisional shelfmarking, the inquirer scanning the shelves for similar material will have a fair chance of spotting the new title, even though it may yet be weeks or months before the LC catalog cards arrive or the full processing of the book can otherwise be completed.

Grant me, again temporarily, the hypothesis that 20 *more* of our 100 patrons might plausibly be expected to resolve their search in this manner. Up to now, we have satisfied 60 out of 100 inquirers, even though the full, formal cataloging and processing may be weeks or months away. To be sure, we may later refine the form of author or the classmark, but there is only a slight probability—say 2 percent in each case—that either refinement will decisively improve the findability of the book.

Let us assume that a set of LC catalog cards now arrives and cannot be filed at once because of a backlog of similar work. Shall we (1) let the book wait its turn, whenever that may come, or (2) establish priorities and try to do first things first?

If, in weighing the priorities, we postulate that getting the temporary author card into the public catalog was worth 40 points and getting the book onto the open shelves with a temporary classmark was worth 20 points, then perhaps getting the title card into the public catalog is worth 15 points; getting the subject cards into the public catalog is worth 15 points; reconciling the subject cards with earlier entries is worth 5 points; replacing the temporary author card with LC's author card is worth 2 points; and filing in the shelflist entry is worth 1 point. Let's see, that makes 98 points, so refining the classmark must be worth 2 points.

I don't ask you to agree with these precise numbers; substitute your own. What I think is important is to make the attempt to weigh the priorities. During the first exciting weeks of a book's life, isn't imperfect access better than no access at all? If it should cost a little more to make the book *available* (for consultation if not for circulation) from the day of its arrival, wouldn't it be worth it?

I like to think of a book as being most valuable when new, and thereafter progressively less valuable. As argued elsewhere in these pages, I suspect that many a book could be said to lose value at the rate of 2 percent a week. At least, there would probably be many a timely book which you would not order at all if you could not have it during its first year of availability. At the end of its first year, even a mint copy offered on a remainder counter at an 80-percent discount might not seem attractive. That being the case, it cannot be an exaggeration to suggest that each week's delay in making the book available is like throwing away 2 percent of what it cost to buy and process it.

Even as regards a less topical book, surely the decision to buy it at all assumes that if bought, it will be used, so that again each week's delay in making it available for use is like throwing away *some* percentage of what it cost.

Now suppose you have a situation in which it has been taking about six weeks from the decision to buy to making the book available to the reader. And suppose you could cut this time to two weeks. If we think of our book as having cost $10 (between purchase price and processing) and as losing value at the rate of 1 or 2 percent a week, then to take six weeks when perhaps two weeks would suffice is to throw away from 4 to 8 percent of the value of the book, or 40 to 80 cents. To salvage this value for the reader would be worth something. Even salvaging *part* of this value through a temporary author card or a provisional shelfmark would be worth something.

In fact, in the case of a timely book, early but sloppy cataloging might serve the readers far better than late but perfect cataloging, with really no disadvantages if provision were made for ultimate correction of initial errors or inconsistencies. As a matter of fact, speaking as a catalog *user*, I doubt I'd be seriously inconvenienced if the inconsistencies stayed in, because the way I as a user approach a subject catalog is diametrically opposite to the way a cataloger approaches it. I am trying to get information *out* of it; the cataloger is trying to put information *into* it.

Confronted with a drawer full of cards of possible interest to me, I pay little or no attention to the cataloger's meticulous efforts to move logically from the general to the particular; I just settle down and pick my way through everything. Oh, I may first run my eye quickly down the dividers, and I may even start with one that seems to narrow the search somewhat. But more often than not, I then go back and skim the rest of the cards anyway.

It isn't that I don't trust the cataloger. It isn't that I don't think someone else could anticipate my question. It is just that I know for sure that a thousand catalogers working a thousand years could not anticipate both the question *and* the information I bring with it. I might say, if asked, "I want a broad general introduction to this topic." But after a personal review of the library's actual holdings, I might contradict myself and make off with a very specific treatment of a very small corner of the subject, for no better reason than that I found the author, title, or topic "interesting," whatever that means.

I know that catalogers *must* fret about whether a given work is most appropriately classifiable under South America, Spanish America, Latin America, Hispano-America, or Ibero-America. But to me as a catalog *user*, most of this is love's labor lost, if the reference to Peru that I am looking for could lie in any of the histories under any of these headings.

John Holt has said that if we taught children to talk the way we teach them to read, they'd never learn. Similarly, if you could teach library users to use the card catalog the way catalogers use it, they'd never get the hang of it, because that isn't the way the mind works. The mind is not without its own logic, but it is not the linear logic of the course outline or of the catalog of subject headings.

One of my old instructors used to say in mock despair, "Here I've told you everything I know and still you know nothing." Exactly. Because I couldn't take in *his* knowledge except in *my* way and in my own time. We might have been working on the same jigsaw puzzle, but if I had fitted together only 100 pieces, only *I* could know which of his 10,000 additional pieces I was ready for next.

I believe that's the way most of us do—and should—use a card catalog or scan open shelves. We should not even try to rely too much on the kind of ex post facto logic that the grammarians use. We should, quite frankly, rely more on serendipity and free association and that potent intangible called "interest."

As long as I was the publisher of *Books in Print*, the *Subject Guide to Books in Print, Paperbound Books in Print, Forthcoming Books, Subject Guide to Forthcoming Books*, and the *American Book Publishing Record*, it might have seemed self-seeking of me to express the following views. But now that I have no further financial interest in them, perhaps I will not be misunderstood if I ask whether our thinking about subject cataloging and union cataloging and system-wide book catalogs has sufficiently taken account of the advent of these book-finding tools. After all, the best of card catalogs leaves much unsaid. It does not list what the library or the system does not own, and it does not tell whether the books listed are on the shelf, in use, or perhaps lost.

By contrast, the *Subject Guide to Books in Print* lists 250,000 titles of 2,000 publishers, whether the library owns the books or not, and does not deny the inquirer the information that a book exists merely because the library has not yet bought it. True, the inquirer may thus learn he wants a book the library doesn't own, but he is surely the richer for knowing his alternatives. And in point of fact, a title not then owned by the library may actually be more quickly accessible than another which is owned but in circulation.

An inquirer comes to the library, scans the shelves without success — and then what? Perhaps the catalog will tell him what might have been on the shelves, but if it isn't there, that may not be much help. If there were a county-wide union catalog in book form, he might be well advised to scan that next, but again his first question may be, "Is there a book that will meet my needs?" rather than, "What does this library or the system of which it is a part happen to own?" Incidentally, if the library could help him identify the book he really needed, it might be doing him a real service, even if he then has to go out and buy it for himself.

I don't probe this line of thinking because I believe card catalogs have no place, but because I do have a feeling that the branches of a large system might be better served with their own copies of the standard in-print reference tools than with book versions of the central catalog at vastly higher cost. I also suspect that when someone brings an inquiry to the Niagara Falls Public Library, the real question is what book will help him, not whether it happens to be owned by the libraries of western New York State. That's secondary.

I suppose I will be asked how I think a new book will find its way into the subject bibliographies prior to availability of the LC cataloging, inasmuch as the editors of those published bibliographies may also be waiting to learn what class numbers and headings LC will assign. It's a good question, and very, very relevant to the *PW* Weekly Record, the *American Book Publishing Record*, and the Wilson *Cumulative Book Index*. These all wait for and use the LC cataloging. Last time I checked, the listings in *PW* were delayed just about 40 days beyond what had been the case before 1960 when *PW* started relying on LC cataloging.

It can be noted, however, that each year the editors of the *Subject Guide to Books in Print* do their own (temporary) assigning of subject headings to many thousands of new titles, since it is either this or leave them out, and they find that LC later picks the same heading about 90 percent of the time. The subject-heading determinations in *Forthcoming Books* and in *Paperbound Books in Print* are also made from publishers' information, before LC has seen the books. They aren't official, but they work.

Approval and Gathering Plans

I am not sure many publishers realize quite what "big business" our research libraries have become. At least I found it an eye-opener to sit in on the second annual International Seminar on Approval and Gathering Plans in Large and Medium Size Academic Libraries in the fall of 1969.

Some 80 librarians attended, none of whom so much as batted an eye when one of their number would tell about authorizing Richard Abel to send them one each of every monograph published in the English language, here or abroad, excepting only fiction and reprints, with supplementary contracts covering everything in German, everything in Russian, everything in French, and so on. Ohio State reported a current book budget of over $1 million and acquisitions of close to 150,000 volumes a year, with 17,000 standing orders for titles in series. In these big leagues they don't "select" books, they "gather" them, and that is what the so-called "gathering plans" are all about.

In general, those who think of these plans as "approval plans" tend to dislike them, whereas those who think of them as "gathering plans" or "blanket ordering plans" tend to like them. The difference in attitude seems to be largely a matter of budget. The big university libraries want all the books and want them early — before there has been time for reviews or redundant faculty requests. They'd rather be reproached for buying unwanted books than for failure to have books when wanted.

Those who cannot buy all the books or anything like it, even in narrowly defined fields, may still be attracted by the "on-approval" concept, but usually have more difficulty making it work. In an approval plan neither buyer nor seller can afford too high a level of returns.

There has been a definite trend toward wider use of gathering plans, especially in university libraries where book money has commonly risen faster than staff, and where the waste involved in buying potentially unwanted books has been weighed against the very tangible expense of screening them out. Carl Jackson, speaking at the ALA Pre-Conference on Acquisitions in 1969, cited estimated savings of $15,000 a year in clerical time and $20,000 a year in faculty and professional time resulting from the simplification of selection procedures inherent in a move to a blanket ordering plan. This was in the context of overall book expenditures of $125,000.

Practice makes perfect. One major university library returned 25 percent of the books received the first season, 18 percent the second year, and only 9 percent the third year. Another university returns less than 5 percent of the books received under its blanket order plans.

Although one faculty member may suggest returning 25 of any 100 titles in his general field of interest, the next member of the same faculty will almost certainly rescue half of the proposed discards, and the pile of books to be returned will get smaller and smaller with each inspection.

Under the most successful plans, it seems indicated that the library staff comes ultimately to respect the supplier's judgment as highly as its own, recognizing, of course, that even its own judgment is never so infallible as to preclude an occasional post-mortem on "why we bought this or didn't buy that."

Success depends primarily on continual refinement of the supplier's instructions. The reasons for each rejection are studied to see how the instructions might have been restated to prevent the submission of that reject.

A typical instruction obliges a supplier to send an approval copy of every title of a defined list of publishers with certain agreed exclusions, such as mysteries, science fiction, pure law, clinical medicine, textbooks, devotionals, how-to books, juveniles, agriculture, cookbooks, reprints, and titles costing more than $50.

The wholesaler who really pioneered in the area of blanket ordering is Richard Abel, of Portland, Oregon. I may do him an injustice if I try to list some of his various services as he explained them to me, since he is constantly enlarging them, but last year his coverage included hardbounds and paperbacks, trade books, and short-discount books—domestic and foreign, documents, pamphlets, you name it. Paperbacks could be ordered prebound. He was beginning to maintain stocks of European titles in his U.S. warehouses and to offer them here at European list prices. Books could be shipped as available or held for inclusion of LC cards. Books could be returned without permission and with no limit on the amount. His staff accepted responsibility for the prevention of duplication between United States and United Kingdom editions and for checking out faculty requests marked "Do not dupe." Library customers could arrange to have books sent without prior notification or authorization, or could ask to receive a notification slip, which is then returned if the book is wanted.

Needless to say, the test of a gathering plan is not whether it provides the best discount, but whether it provides the books. Abel's pricing policy, as he described it to the group at Kalamazoo, is basically a "cost-plus" policy—his cost plus $1.20, or $1.50, or $1.80, or something like that. This way his prices may be noticeably lower than conventional pricing on the higher-priced books and perhaps "list-plus" on inexpensive books.

Libraries may write exceptions into their blanket orders covering certain long-standing direct-buying or exchange relationships, and may write separate blanket orders covering books of domestic origin, English-language imports, German books, French books, Spanish books, and so on. Since books are sent on approval, no actual order need be placed until a book is in hand, so that funds are never encumbered until it is certain that they will be spent.

Some librarians have been skeptical about blanket order plans, which have seemed to them an abdication of a responsibility, namely book selection, that is the very heart and soul of librarianship. They could envisage only an abrupt decline in the quality of their collections. They said: "Surely any selection left to a profit-oriented bookdealer will inevitably be weighted in favor of the books that make him the greatest profit or the least trouble. Surely there cannot help but be a subtle but significant gap between what we want to buy and what he wants to sell."

Some still feel this way and indeed can cite experience. Any publisher's sales manager can cite examples of pressure by library book wholesalers aimed at persuading him that they have the power to diminish his sales to libraries if he does not give them special discount treatment.

Many librarians, however, have come to believe that their control

111

over the quality of their collections can be increased rather than downgraded through the aid of effective blanket order plans. For one thing, the new books arrive earlier. The collection is fresher, more current. The books are in hand when the reviews break.

Also, the staff can do less plodding and more planning; it can back off from the trees and get a better look at the woods. Its continually refined instructions to the supplier may represent a definition of its goals vastly superior to anything ever before available to its inside book selectors.

The greatest gain, however, seems to lie in the way the suppliers have risen to their new responsibilities. Formerly they could feel that they'd done their part when they had sent what they could and reported on the balance. One wholesaler, when reproached for falsely reporting books as out of stock, told the protesting publisher, "When I don't get the discount I want, I don't stock 'em, and when I don't stock 'em, they certainly are out of stock with me, aren't they?"

Any wholesaler who accepts a blanket order contract, however, accepts a new (and defined) type of responsibility. Like the library book-selection staff itself, he may have for the first time a really precise definition of what the library wants from him — and means to get. And he will be up against a staff with time to spend making sure they get it.

He may also sense a new mandate regarding speed of delivery. Under the former policy of waiting for the reviews and the faculty recommendations, and cumulating them, and weighing them, and then perhaps cumulating the resulting orders, the supplier could be forgiven for assuming that if he didn't get the order for several months after publication, perhaps no one would mind if he took another month to supply. Under the new policy he comes to realize that acceptable performance means shipping each new and relevant book the day he himself gets it — before the library staff starts asking where it is.

One of the most frequently cited advantages of the blanket order plans is their speed. This comes, as mentioned above, from *not* waiting for reviews. If you've never done so, it could be interesting to check up once in a while to see how often you'd be sorry if you made your first round of selections just from the publishers' advance book information without waiting for independent appraisals. Once you know author, title, subject, publisher, and timing, you know quite a lot.

The advantages of speed are, however, what you make of them. In a situation where books are normally held out of use until the arrival of the LC catalog cards, more speed might just amount to a policy of "hurry up and wait."

On close consideration, it seems to be true that wholesalers have always had a certain power to modify library book selection decisions. They clearly have it when a library, nearing the end of its fiscal year, sends in a list of $1,500 worth of books with orders to supply any $1,000 worth. They clearly have it in their capacity to be chronically out of stock on anything they would rather not handle. For the library, the line of least resistance is just to order something else.

Wholesalers have it in their capacity to report that they simply do not carry a certain item or line. In theory the library will then order it elsewhere. In practice this kind of direct ordering may stand aside for more urgent work—until it hardly seems important any more.

In a blanket ordering situation it is absolutely essential to keep some kind of watch—at least a spot check—on what's coming that isn't wanted, or not coming that is wanted. But then this always was desirable, except that before it wasn't always done.

Blanket ordering, or the "category" approach to book selection as some prefer to call it, is not for everyone. One wholesaler believes that it may not be applicable where the budget is under $75,000 or in public and school library systems, where the problem is "how many of some" rather than "one each of many."

Although there are similarities between the blanket ordering plans and the so-called Greenaway plans, the details and objectives are somewhat different. Some years ago Emerson Greenaway of the Philadelphia Public Library began asking the major publishers to send an early copy of every book they published, so his staff could have the book in hand when making its decisions about buying additional copies. His staff had been receiving a certain number of free review copies, but could never be sure which they'd get and which they'd miss. They might, perhaps, have asked to receive all titles on an approval basis, but the need to return the unwanted books would have been burdensome to library and publishers alike. A plan was therefore worked out under which the library would receive everything and pay for it, and in exchange for its commitment not to return anything, it was to receive a much larger discount than usual, perhaps 60 or 75 percent off list. The logic was that the library would save enough on the books it wanted to justify discarding the others.

Greenaway plans were developed for, and are really only appropriate for, large city systems like Philadelphia. Many publishers have agreed to work with large libraries on this basis, but their follow-through has often been poor. In some cases the Greenaway copies have been shipped so late as to make them useless for selection purposes. In some cases one department of a large publishing house has sent its titles promptly and consistently, but other departments have fallen down. In at least one situation the instructions to ship the Greenaway copies early fell afoul of another policy of long standing under which wholesalers' orders were shipped before retailers', retailers' before libraries', and large orders before small orders. There may be a trend away from Greenaway plans, i.e., away from selection procedures which can be jeopardized by spotty performance on the part of the publishers.

The assumption underlying the Greenaway plans, namely that the selection process benefits by having the book in hand, may possibly be less valid than it at first appeared. A children's picture book can perhaps be appraised on sight or within a few minutes, but any attempt to read and appraise full-length books would require major involvement of a large staff. It must be seldom that a staff member's reading and appraisal of a full-length book could make an important difference in the selection decision. After all, one of the basic questions is not how readers will feel about the book after they have read it, but whether they will ask to read it. They'll make that decision on the basis of the title, the author, the publicity, the reviews, etc., and the selector who is trying to serve them might do worse than base his decision on the same factors. A staff review, however valid, isn't going to be nearly as *relevant* as the review in *Time*.

A basic problem with Greenaway plans is that they just don't fit anywhere in the publishers' fulfillment procedures. Up at the policy-making level, the goal is "give the customer what he wants." Down at the operating level, standing orders under a Greenaway plan, or some similar plan, are, as one big publisher candidly admits, "a pain in the neck." They are neither fish nor fowl. They are like review copies, except that they aren't because they have to be billed. They are like ordinary prepub orders from wholesalers, booksellers, and individuals, except that there are complaints unless they are handled ahead of these other orders. The discount is such an exception to all rules that Greenaway orders require special routing through the billing department.

The biggest problem of all is setting up a foolproof mechanism for *telling* the order department to send each book. Order departments are set up for one purpose, to fill orders arriving from *outside* the department. No orders from outside, no action. By rights, Greenaway copies ought to be ordered sent by the same person who orders the review copies sent, but because one instruction is only a "ship" instruction and the other is a "ship and bill" instruction, the internal routine prescribes that the "ship and bill" instructions be issued from the sales department, not the publicity department. Thus far we are talking as if only the trade department were involved. At least 40 percent of the new titles emanate from departmentalized companies where an order to ship and bill a college department book would have to start in the college department, and the same for the elementary-high school department, the mail-order-book department, and so forth.

I really think it's probably a losing game to expect publishers—more than a few, anyway—to do anything that is outside their regular basic routines. It's hard enough to get one wholesaler to serve you the way you want to be served, without trying to get 30 or 130 publishers all doing the same thing your way.

Besides, Greenaway copies are single-copy orders, and it ought to be one of the fundamental long-term goals of any rational book-distribution system to avoid burdening the publisher with single-copy orders. If 50 publishers were to operate Greenaway plans with 50 large libraries, covering 5,000 new titles a year, that would be 250,000 individual packages shipped and billed. If the same distribution were to be handled through wholesalers, the publishers would be shipping in bulk to the wholesalers, and the wholesalers would be shipping in bulk to the libraries. Each library might get just one or two combined shipments a week, an enormous saving in packaging and paper work. If I were a publisher anxious to cooperate with a large library interested in Greenaway plan service, I certainly think I'd try to work it out through that library's chosen wholesaler rather than direct. A possible alternative would be for the publishers to set up some kind of cooperative to take care of this kind of distribution.

Speaking of publishing cooperatives, the Dutch have an interesting co-op that might be worth our study in this country. It is set up specially to handle single-copy orders. The Dutch booksellers are entirely free to order single copies direct from the publisher, but if they prefer, they can make one order out of what would otherwise be several orders to several publishers and send it to the Central Book House. The discount they get is minimal, but what makes the system work is the fact that it is the policy of the Central Book House to stock *every title of every participating publisher.*

I believe the system works approximately as follows, or at least did when I visited the Central Book House a few years ago, at which time the co-op was celebrating its twentieth year of operation. All

transactions are at list price less 25 percent—i.e., the publishers sell
to the co-op at list less 25, and the booksellers buy from the co-op at
list less 25. The expenses of operation, which run about 13 percent,
are then divided among the cooperators in proportion to the use they
make of the service. I believe the publishers pay 9 percent and the
booksellers 4 percent, or something like that.

The Central Book House as it operates in Holland is used, I believe, only by booksellers. If we had one here, perhaps it could be used
by booksellers and libraries alike. It would be a mistake, I think, to
set up such a service in a way that would take business from the
wholesalers; the main idea would be to relieve the publishers of the
burden of supplying single copies of the books the wholesalers prefer
not to handle. It would be a facility deliberately set up to handle the
kinds of orders nobody else wanted, and therefore its discounts would
be very small, but you'd go there only when speed and simplicity were
more important to you than discount. Attempting such a thing for all
titles of all publishers might be too ambitious to begin with, but such
a service could probably be useful even if it embraced only the titles
of a limited number of publishers. You'd know before you ordered
whether the publisher was participating, and you'd know that if he
was, then all his titles would be stocked. If such a service existed, it
would probably be an ideal agent for handling Greenaway plans.

The Case against Central Ordering and Processing

There is a strong tendency in all large systems of any kind to centralize, sometimes for good and sufficient reason, but often just on the unexamined assumption that centralization is "efficient." Long-unexamined assumptions are always worth fresh examination, however. "If you have always done it that way, it must be wrong." Or, as Thoreau says, "They govern best who govern least."

Parkinson's law works just as inexorably in library systems as in business: "Work expands to fill the time available for doing it." "Centralization" often becomes a euphemism for duplication.

In a typical case, the branch library sends its order to "central." Central accumulates and integrates the orders of many branches and sends them to the supplier, who sends the books back to central. Central then breaks them down for reshipment to the branches. Sometimes the routine is branch-to-central-to-regional-to-supplier-to-regional-to-central-to-branch. Not uncommonly it even becomes branch-to-central-to-city buying office-to-co-op-to-supplier-to-processer-to-supplier-to-central-to-branch.

How else would you handle it? Well, what would be wrong with letting the branch order *directly* from the supplier, and preferably from a supplier known to carry stock of both books and processing kits?

If you can think of a thousand reasons why that wouldn't work, think again. It *does* work in many places. In fact, it works extremely well. It puts more responsibility on the librarians down on the firing line — and they love it. Your supplier may cut your discount by 2 percent to cover himself for having to deliver to many places instead of just one — but 2 percent will be less than 10 cents a book, and you can't even relay the orders for 10 cents a book, let alone unpack and redistribute the shipments.

It is sometimes feared that decentralized ordering will lead to lack of "control." It needn't. You can still do your basic bargaining with your suppliers on a centralized basis. You can make the supplier responsible (if this seems necessary) for not letting the branches overshoot their budgets. You can even hold him responsible for supplying only "approved" books, though any such infringement on the judgment of your own branch librarians does make them feel you don't trust them very far.

Cataloging may be something you don't want your branches to get involved in, but there are suppliers who will supply the books either completely preprocessed or with cataloging kits ready for local processing, and chances are your branches would rather paste in their own pockets than accept the delays inherent in having it done for them. There are useful economies to be made in the centralized *printing* of cards and kits, but less advantage in centralized jacketing and pasting in of pockets and spine labels.

In setting up the lines of procurement, the value of *time* warrants consideration ahead of everything else. No library ever ought to settle for a period longer than two weeks between sensing the need for a book and having it in service, and there ought to be provision for moving faster than this in case of need. There are areas where most bookstores and some libraries phone today and have the book tomorrow; more libraries could have similar service if they demanded it.

Of course, the goal of having books in service within two weeks of deciding to buy them pretty well rules out "custom" processing at another place. To get consistent speed, the library must order from a place known to maintain extensive stocks, and it must (1) stand ready to accept the standard processing offered by that source, (2) stand ready to accept book-with-cataloging-kit, or (3) stand ready to accept the book only and do its own cataloging and processing.

If the library tries to buy the books from one place and have them processed at another, it'll never get them in two weeks. *And yet nothing is gained by letting the process take longer.* Obviously time is lost, and usually money as well.

Nothing but unacceptable delay can come from any attempt to deal with a commercial source that does not carry stock and that orders only on receipt of an order—or through a processing center which also maintains no stock. There may be times when delay is acceptable, as when the books ordered at the end of the spring school term are not even required until the reopening of school in the fall, but even here the orders placed in June could, many of them, have been placed in January, February, and March for delivery in January, February, or March, with real gain to the educational situation.

Let us review once again the common assumption that centralization leads to economy. It is true that a wholesaler will bid higher on business that involves high multiples of the same titles and can be billed and shipped to one recipient. It is true that he may offer a lesser discount if asked to accept small orders directly from individual branches and schools, with direct shipment. (It is easier for him to pick titles in tens or thirties than to pick them in ones.)

However, the surcharges, such as they might be, for dealing directly with individual libraries as against dealing with a central ordering and receiving operation are almost certain to be less than the extra cost of doing within the system the cumulating of orders and the breaking down of shipments. The important thing is to weigh the internal costs against the external costs and to know just how the costs break.

I would offer it as a basic premise that paper work costs more within a nonprofit governmental organization than within a commercial organization. The difference can be startling. It would not be difficult to find cases where the extra cost of bringing orders together centrally, ordering centrally, receiving centrally, and distributing from a central point (ignoring processing, if any), works out as high as 50 cents or even $1 per book, as against 10 cents or so to let the wholesaler do it.

It is not even as certain as often assumed that wholesalers prefer large orders to small ones. Beyond a certain limit the economies of size are negligible. In dealing with fairly large systems, it is probably true to say that a wholesaler would definitely prefer to receive orders weekly or monthly throughout the year than to receive a huge annual or semiannual order. There is no wholesaler so big that he could accept a year's cumulated orders from a large city and fill them immediately, and this is doubly true if the order hits him in company with a large number of similar orders. Wholesalers and, incidentally, publishers who sell direct, have their heavy months and their light months, and it will pay library customers to know when those light months are and think about the possibility of enjoying the better service that would come from taking advantage of this knowledge. Much of the delay, incidentally, in acquiring books comes from passing the order through the double jeopardy of a lengthy cumulation period in the library system and then having it go through a lengthy fulfillment period in the wholesaler's.

What is the case for cooperative (nonprofit) central processing? What have we learned from the numerous "experiments" that have been made in recent years?

One man who has made some fairly detailed studies of these experiments is Walter Curley, formerly Director of Information Systems at Arthur D. Little and Company. Speaking at the ALA Pre-Conference on Acquisitions in June 1969, he said:

> Running your own centralized processing operation is a very difficult task. It can be done, and it is being done quite well by a number of agencies. It is also being done rather badly by even more, and there are quite a few cases where central processing operations have gone up in smoke because of the problems involved.

A problem which particularly tends to plague noncommercial processing centers is that of increasing costs, not just because of inflation, which presumably affects commercial firms as well, but because of civil service obstacles to hiring the most competent or firing the least competent. There is also an unmistakable tendency to hire (or inherit) overqualified people.

Noncommercial centers also tend to rush in where commercial operators would fear to tread, i.e., where the group to be served is simply too small to permit efficient mechanization. Any attempt to provide central processing for a group of 10 or 15 libraries with a combined volume of 25,000 or 50,000 books a year — even with reasonable unification of standards, which is by no means always permitted — is probably foredoomed to failure.

In general, those cooperative processing centers which have been successful in the sense that they have at least survived their first few years are those still enjoying a subsidy of some kind. After four years of operation at the Wyoming State Library's Processing Center, for example, Paul Cors could only report with unusual candor that "successes seem to have the upper hand at last," but he added that he was by no means certain that Wyoming's local libraries would continue to use the State Processing Center *if they had to pay for its services*, i.e., if its LSCA subsidy dried up.

There has been a tendency to say: "Well, if success depends on putting together an operation of a certain minimum size, then let's plan accordingly. Let's combine counties or even small states as necessary to reach that size."

The rub seems to be that as a co-op gains members, the difficulties of pleasing all of them seem to mount faster than the economies. In theory a computer can be programmed to consult the preferences of each customer before printing out each catalog card or pocket or spine label, and can give everyone the exact treatment he has specified as regards the spine labeling of biographies, the location of call numbers, etc.

In practice each increment of computer versatility comes only at a price—a price not only for added initial programming, but also expressed in added rental for added memory or added components. Computer specialists always cheerfully say, "No problem," when asked about things which in actual fact may imply another $1,000 a month in extra rentals. (It may be no problem for *them*, but it can be a problem for *you* if that extra versatility is going to be called into play only 1,000 times a month, and thus saddle you with an extra $1 cost for every time you use it.)

Some of the talk about the MARC II magnetic tapes would lead you to believe that if you had subscribed to the 1970 series, your computer would then be able to give you on demand a set of LC cards for any of the '70 series, headed according to your specifications. Maybe so. But for action one iota faster than old hand methods, would you believe $10,000 *a month* in computer rentals just for openers? Not counting the initial programming, because the MARC tapes are just data, not programming.

Although the cost of computer memory is rather steadily coming down, another approach to the problem of rapid access to LC cataloging may yet beat out the computer approach. I am referring to microfiche. It will probably always be cheaper to acquire, store, and retrieve *seldom-used* data in microform rather than in digital magnetic storage. Microfiche as a cataloging data base is so promising that any plan for centralized processing that did not take account of it might want to be rethought. In some cases, it may mean that libraries too small to think of tackling their own computerized cataloging might nevertheless be able to handle their own microfiche cataloging and thus avoid the delays inherent in going to an outside processing service.

If I seem to be somewhat anticomputer—well, the impression is accurate. In my opinion, though I have used it successfully, the computer is probably the most oversold piece of hardware in the history of technology. Computers have undeniably doubled the time it takes

121

publishers to fill an order, and they will double what it costs *you* in time and money to place and process an order, if you let them. Unless you are a glutton for punishment, content yourself with refining your manual operations unless and until you find someone else who has successfully (i.e., with demonstrable gains in time and money) computerized problems so exactly like yours that you can reasonably arrange to use his programs without change.

As of now there are just three approaches to computerization: (1) you bring in outside experts and they know so little of library problems their work is useless; (2) you *don't* bring in outside experts, but when you also fail by reason of not having on the staff the kind of programming talent that commands the $50,000-a-year salaries paid by the software houses, you are told you should have used more outside help; (3) by great good luck you build a team embracing high-level expertise in both disciplines, and it advises you that in the present state of the art you have more to gain from ordinary, old-fashioned work simplification than from computerization.

Is there, nevertheless, a case for central processing?

If all goes well with New York State's ANYLTS (Association of New York Libraries for Technical Services) program, the state's 22 major public library systems, serving 727 libraries and 298 branches, will eventually (perhaps by 1975) funnel all their book orders through a single acquisition and cataloging operation and will receive cards and processed books through the nearest of several regional processing centers.

Joseph Eisner, director of ANYLTS, says cautiously:

> It is not anticipated that customers will enjoy any substantial increase in wholesale discount, or in speed of delivery. . . . However, they will receive more timely reports on the status of orders . . . complete financial accounting by book fund . . . improvement of interloan through timely production of consolidated holdings listings . . . release to other duties of staff currently involved in cataloging and acquisitions. . . .

Initially ANYLTS will serve only public library systems, and will handle only English-language books. Eventually it will "consider" the production of book catalogs, the servicing of academic and public school libraries, perhaps the retrospective computerization of existing union catalogs, and the servicing of its members with systems analysis and programming in the areas of circulation and serials control.

Needless to say, the private firms offering processing services take a dim view of most cooperative central processing schemes,

charging that on the record the promised economies never materialize. Costs are higher and service lower, they say, despite subsidies
and tax exemption and (usually) all kinds of compromise with the
kind of performance that is demanded of the commercial processors.

Since the decision on whether to join a "system" may be one of
the most far-reaching that an acquisitions librarian will face in the
years ahead, it may be useful to review the arguments pro and con.

The road to solid regional agreement on cooperative acquisition
and processing is, of course, a rocky one at best. It would be my guess
that any cooperative system attempting to serve a group of libraries
not under a unified control will have its problems. Being a cooperative, it will be the prisoner of the desires of its members and will have
to try to give them service beyond what they could get from commercial channels, and this will drive up its costs until the members willing to settle for less customization find it cheaper to pull out and go to
a commercial source, which in turn will leave the cooperative with
progressively less desirable business to perform. Success will heavily
depend on the capacity to knock heads together, as, for example,
when a common source of important money can say to the recipients,
"Play ball or no more money," or where it is possible to dangle new
money, such as a federal grant, before the eyes of the proposed participants to the point where they will say, "Well, it's not our money and
it won't cost us anything to look."

By rights, "looking" *should* lead to "buying," at least if the promised economies materialize. The promised economies, however, usually depend pretty much on the following assumptions: (1) that the
Library of Congress will finally get (and keep) its cataloging really
current and complete; (2) that the cooperating libraries will agree to
unify their cataloging practices; and (3) that the cooperating libraries
will agree to uniform processing.

To claim, as was claimed in the Nelson study, that the current
book-processing costs of 22 New York library systems could be reduced by 32 cents per volume, *provided a tax-exempt co-op had the
three above-mentioned advantages*, was not to claim very much! In
fact, greater economies still would probably be gladly offered by any
commercial processor if he could count on those three advantages!

Economy, then, is probably not a valid argument for cooperative
acquisition-and-processing, and in fact Joe Eisner of ANYLTS (unlike
Nelson Associates) does not offer it as an argument. What he stresses
is improved service, notably improved status reporting.

Service is definitely something money can buy, provided the buyer makes it clear that he wants it and is prepared to pay for it. Per-

haps the most serious area of misunderstanding between librarians and their commercial suppliers is that too often (according to the suppliers) librarians *say* they want service but take the low bid regardless. (Librarians tend to say that they want service *and* would happily pay for it, if they just knew how to specify it to the satisfaction of their contracting officers.) It would be an irony if the real justification for going co-op was to find a way around burdensome low-bid requirements and make it practical to buy service, not just discount.

It is often assumed that a co-op must inevitably save money inasmuch as it: (1) need pay no taxes; (2) need pay no interest on borrowed money; and (3) need pay no high executive salaries or profits.

The first argument is unimportant. The taxes paid by a commercial wholesaler, though 50 percent of his profits, may be only 3 percent of his prices. Furthermore, what's good about reducing taxes? Isn't that where library book appropriations come from?

The second argument is simply fallacious. Whether a processing center is financed by federal, state, local, or private borrowing, interest will have to be paid on the money borrowed.

As to salary levels, the top man in a private company does often make more, between salary and profit participation (though perhaps with less security), than his opposite number in a government agency, but overall salary costs may be lower. For example, work done by four professionals under civil service might be done by one professional and three nonprofessionals in a competitive situation.

At first glance, nonprofit operations are "clean"; commercial operations are contaminated by the profit motive. ("Socialism is good, capitalism is bad.") In practice, socialism can be surprisingly inefficient and capitalism can be at least comparatively efficient. If you fret sometimes over the fact that your present choice of suppliers often seems a choice between bad and worse, rather than between good and better, you might ponder how bad it could be if you had no choice at all.

Co-ops have their problems, too—big problems. They may begin with high hopes, a nice starting subsidy, an imaginative and dedicated director, the necessary minimum volume of work from one or two of the larger cooperators, and a willingness on the part of everyone not to demand immediate miracles. What counts, though, is what happens when the subsidy ends, the dedicated director moves on, patience turns to impatience, and one of the major participants pulls out.

It may almost be a law of nature that in any integration of the work of several systems, the least efficient will gain most, and the most efficient will gain least. The fellow who gains least will inevitably be disappointed and may demand special favors, or even threaten to pull out. Either way, costs then rise for the others, perhaps bringing someone else to the point of dissatisfaction.

Co-ops also tend to be disappointing when it comes to speed. Too often they are simply an added link in the chain of events, lengthening procedures twice: once in the ordering, again in the fulfillment. They learn the hard way what scores of publishers have had to learn before them, namely, that when manual processes are replaced by machine processes, all too often daily cycles become (for "efficiency") weekly cycles.

If one then concedes what Joe Eisner of ANYLTS concedes, namely, that neither dollar savings nor time savings can be counted on too heavily, what then remains as the attraction? The glittering promise at the end of the trail is really "automation," the automated status reports, the automated catalog, the fully integrated area catalog, perhaps in book-catalog form, perhaps open to interrogation via closed-circuit TV.

This kind of vista is exciting, certainly, but there are more ways to gather the data than as a by-product of acquisition and processing. In fact, the introduction of International Standard Book Numbering provides a beautifully simple means whereby all the libraries in an area could notify a central source of their latest acquisitions.

The veritable prototype of central processing schemes is of course LC's Card Division. Unhappily it still, after 70 years, leaves much to be desired. Even titles given a high priority were taking (last time I asked) two weeks to be cataloged and two weeks more to be printed, and other books take much longer, though the whole world be waiting. The MARC II magnetic tapes, intended to expedite the transmission of the cataloging information, deliver most of their data about 12 weeks late, and, according to one would-be user, there are currently unpredictable errors of some kind in about every fifth entry, apparently representing an error of transcription from the Title II cards.

To be sure, there are plans for expediting LC's cataloging through cataloging-in-source, with the goal of covering about 10,000 titles by the end of 1971. It is said that this should expedite the production of the Title II catalog cards (on these titles only) by about two weeks.

If all goes well, then, LC catalog cards will be available on 10,000 titles within two weeks—and on 90,000 other titles after several months. Meanwhile those who need the information will either wait, and wait, and wait, or duplicate the cataloging themselves, or devise schemes for putting the books into circulation prior to processing.

If there is to be any serious talk of cooperative central processing, will it not make sense to concentrate first, before anything else, on bringing at least *one* such project, namely, LC cataloging, to successful operation? If it is utopian to press for completion of *all* LC cataloging within two weeks, then it is doubly utopian to expect much from cooperative projects which must depend on LC.

In some ways, the case for cooperative regional processing may be somewhat like the case for the 3-M Company's first big computer years ago. The story may be apocryphal but I like it. It seems they went into their computer program with exceptional caution and care and made sure they were simplifying their paper work, not just automating it. They laid down a rule that *no* paper was to be recopied merely because it was crossing departmental lines. And after two years of hard preparatory work the president of 3-M was able to report to the stockholders that the computer program was already showing substantial savings — though the computer itself would not be delivered for another year.

It may be some years before cooperative regional processing arrives on your doorstep, but if you prepare ahead of time — if you reduce your ordering procedures to "one writing," if you stop making any but the most essential change in the LC cataloging you buy and really try to use it the way it comes, if you seek out and find a way to pay for the best of the services offered by the best of the commercial suppliers — you may find yourself actually enjoying benefits that others are still only dreaming about.

The Problem of LC Cataloging

By rights the acquisition of Library of Congress catalog cards should be the easy part of the book acquisition process. The catalog cards should routinely come before the book or with the book; certainly the book should never have to wait for the catalog cards. That would be an inexcusable case of the tail wagging the dog. Unfortunately, the tail so commonly wags the dog in this respect that we have pretty much come to accept it.

I would like to think that the problem was going to be solved through cataloging-in-source, now being revived, but I must confess that I am far from sanguine about this. I do believe that the publishers, or at any rate those publishers whose primary business is publishing, will do everything in their power to make it work. I am, however, genuinely fearful that LC will let us down—again.

After all, the MARC II program was to solve the problem and has not done so. Then the current automation program that begins with the catalog card order form was to solve the problem, but seems to have bogged down short of Phase II. The very fact that cataloging-in-source is again being discussed seems a tacit admission that automation isn't expected to solve the problem after all.

Let's back off and see just what we really want. Ideally a set of catalog cards should arrive with or before the book. If they could come *in* the book, fine. But it would seem quite acceptable also if they could be ordered at the same time as the book and arrive in the same mail, give or take a day or two.

I am not arguing against cataloging-in-source, i.e., against having the information on the copyright page of the book. But the fact is that if we do the cataloging promptly enough to get it into the book, there should be no problem about getting printed cards, either. After all, it should not take longer to print the cards than to print and bind the book!

Neither am I arguing against making the cataloging available in the form of magnetic dots on the MARC II tapes, but even in those few libraries automated to the point of being able to utilize information received in this form, the information will not be helpful if not received promptly, and at present the average MARC II entry is many weeks late.

The problem does not lie in distributing the cataloging, but rather in doing the cataloging to begin with, and it is not a new problem. After earlier probes into the possibilities of cataloging-in-source had come to naught, I proposed in 1959 another approach, namely, printing the LC cataloging in the Weekly Record of the *Publishers' Weekly*. The idea was that *PW* and LC would work together to make sure that LC got the earliest possible cataloging copies of the new books, and LC would give a clear priority to the 15,000 to 20,000 new titles that would be listed in the Weekly Record; cards for these books would be ready by the time the *PW* entry was set in type, printed, and received by subscribers.

So that the plan would not significantly delay the listings in *PW*, the goal which John Cronin and I set for ourselves was a maximum of 72 hours for the production of LC's cataloging on any title for which *PW* was known to be waiting. It never happened. Last time I checked, that 72 hours had grown to about 40 *days*. At that time there was a time interval of about 40 days from receipt of the book at the Bowker offices to receipt of the cataloging from LC, and another interval of about 20 days from receipt of the cataloging at Bowker to its appearance in a published issue of *PW*.

To the best of my information, the MARC tapes haven't helped, and a library cataloger who tried to rely on them could find himself waiting three months or more beyond the time his library received the book. Every library in America is therefore right up the same well-known creek today as for the past seven decades. If it elects to wait for the LC cataloging, it can wait for months. And if it decides not to wait, the LC card may arrive tomorrow.

I am not suggesting that LC likes the delays. As a matter of fact, John Cronin and I had conference after conference trying to find answers. I made it my business to make sure the publishers were sending him listing copies as soon as these were sent to *PW*. If necessary, the *PW* listing copies were sent to LC. We worked out a punched-card scheme for spotting the books which had arrived at *PW* but not yet at LC.

The plain fact was, though, that whereas any one book could at any time be pushed through the cataloging process in 72 hours, this only meant a longer wait for the others. In a decade of trying, neither I nor John Cronin ever found a way of achieving a 72-hour cataloging cycle for all the books, or even for just the ones scheduled for listing in the *PW* Weekly Record, though there was occasional agreement that the latter might perhaps warrant priority treatment, inasmuch as there were probably a hundred times as many people waiting for them. The question must be asked: How long, O Lord, how long must we all either duplicate LC's work, or wish we had?

LC's stock explanation is "lack of funds." That won't wash. For 70 years *LC has cataloged all the books;* it merely catalogs them about 90 days late. With all the federal money that has been available the past few years, I find it inconceivable that a hard-nosed plan for catching up on this cataloging wouldn't have been approved in a rush.

Another alibi is: "But there *is* a plan — a plan to computerize the whole card operation. True, it doesn't seem to be working out very well, but if you could see its defects in advance, you should have spoken up." As a matter of fact, I did speak up, and I submitted some alternate proposals, but the main point is that the best method in the world for making cards can't start until you have the cataloging.

The basic trouble with LC cataloging is that the matter of promptness has never been given an adequate priority. Promptness is attainable. There is no mystery about what it would take to get the work done promptly. You just have to make the administrative decision that things are going to get caught up, and stay caught up, *or else* — or else, some heads will roll and be replaced with heads that can follow a directive when given one.

Cataloging-in-source is a great idea, but it must be said that if we had it, we wouldn't need it. Before we can arrange to have cataloging-in-source, we must obviously arrange to catalog promptly; and if we can arrange to catalog promptly, there should be no problem about getting catalog card sets without copying them off copyright pages.

Cataloging-in-source is sometimes discussed as if the problem were one of getting publisher cooperation. In my opinion this is no problem. Publishers were prompt to cooperate in putting LC card numbers on their copyright pages. They will put on additional information *if* it is supplied to them when they have to have it. At least, I believe you can reasonably count on the major publishers and the more professional minor publishers to do everything in their power to comply. They won't succeed 100 percent of the time, of course. It may be impractical to comply as regards some books printed on a rush schedule, or books with very small pages, or books without separate copyright pages, or books printed abroad. It would be foolish even to talk about cataloging-in-source unless something less than 100 percent compliance were to be regarded as worth the effort. The big breakthrough will not come with getting the cataloging on the copyright page; the big breakthrough will come with getting the cataloging *early enough to put on the copyright page*, whether you put it there or not.

If it be assumed that the goals of cataloging-in-source are compatible with the publisher cooperation that can reasonably be expected, the only other problem is what action would be required to enable LC to do its part. It is sometimes assumed that the answer is simply Money. I must say I don't think the answer is this simple. There *are* parameters within which speed costs money, and money can buy speed. It is not necessarily true, however, that a daily newspaper pays more for its editorial work or type composition than a monthly. In fact, it may pay less. Within rather wide limits, the price of speed is planning, not money.

A couple of years ago I proposed to LC that Bowker take over on subcontract LC's cataloging of the current titles that constitute the *PW* Weekly Record, with the understanding that personnel designated by LC could double-check every card. My strategy was going to be to work ahead—to try and get the cataloging provisionally complete and accurate before receipt of the finished book. It would then only be necessary to make one final check of cataloging against book to make sure everything was in order. The proposal was, I grant, somewhat impertinent. Anything Bowker could have done, LC could have done.

The fact remains, LC wasn't doing it and isn't doing it—and should be. It is nonsense to argue that you cannot work ahead on cataloging. Working only from the publishers' early announcements, you can usually (tentatively) verify the author's full name and date of birth, series, LC card number and/or ISBN, and make provisional decisions about class numbers and subject headings. I grant that there isn't any element that *may* not have to be corrected once you have the finished book in hand, but it ought to be possible to substantiate and release a high percentage of such advance work with only the most perfunctory review of final title page, copyright page, contents, pagination, and so forth. As a matter of fact, *unless* this kind of working ahead is practical, cataloging-in-source is out of the question.

I have been told that I clearly "know nothing of cataloging" if I imagine that one can safely attempt advance determinations of class numbers or subject headings without the book at hand. Nonsense! Every year since 1956 the editors of the *Subject Guide to Books in Print* have had to guess at what subject heading LC would eventually assign to about 5,000 very recent or forthcoming books, and every year their guesses have later turned out to be about 90 percent accurate. (Nor were the other 10 percent necessarily misleading, though, to be completely honest, I suppose I should mention the book of poetry entitled *Prefabrications* which got entered under Construction, Concrete.)

Is anyone shocked by the admission that 10 percent of 5,000 new titles may appear each year in the *Subject Guide* under a heading other than LC's final first choice? Don't be. If users never find them, they are no worse off than they would be if the titles had simply been left out, and the users may well find them. In any case, the heading is corrected in the next edition.

I would repeat: All the titles that get into *Books to Come* and the other advance indexes should be cataloged in advance, subject to one final check with the finished book in hand. Maybe a few will offer last-minute problems that cannot be solved out of hand, but surely a high percentage should be able to be finally corrected and released for printing within 24 hours of receipt of the earliest finished book. The final correction process should also take care of rounding out MARC II data, ready for simultaneous release.

In fact, I see no reason why at least 15,000 new books a year shouldn't be thus provisionally cataloged in advance, and why 14,000 of them shouldn't be printed and in distribution within 48 hours of receipt of the actual book.

By contrast, what actually happens? I have already given you my own figures for 1968, showing an average 40-day gap between receipt of a new book at Bowker and receipt of the LC cataloging. More recently, Bill Welch at LC told me that high-priority titles were taking 11 days to go through the cataloging process and 14 days to go through the printing and distribution process — a total of 25 days. For other books, he said, the cataloging time averaged 35½ days and the printing and distribution process took "longer" (than 14 days). He added that it was taking 7 days to fill orders for the cards, once they became available, and that about 60 percent of the cards being ordered were supplied in the first shipment.

Taking this at its face value (though I am not sure Bill Welch himself takes these figures at face value, knowing the tendency of subordinates to tell you what you want to hear), it seems clear that even the high-priority books are averaging 32 days from receipt of book to first shipment of finished cards, which means that half of them are taking longer than 32 days. Is this acceptable? Would it be acceptable if the time could be shaved to 20 days or 15 days? (Remember, we are talking about "high-priority" books.)

I submit that the goal should be 48 hours. If the afternoon news-papers can have the noon Wall Street quotations on the street by 3 P.M., day in and day out, then there is clearly no mechanical reason why we can't have 48-hour service for getting finished catalog cards on at least the high-priority titles, which let's define as the ones that appear in *Books to Come.*

I am not suggesting that this would be possible the way the work is now handled at LC. Last time I asked, I was told that every book moved through something like 27 stages.

I wasn't surprised. I once worked for the federal government myself and was astonished to find that it took six weeks just for a purchase order to work its way from me at the Treasury Department to my opposite number in the Government Printing Office. I followed such an order once; whether by coincidence or pursuant to some ar-cane law, it also passed through 27 stages en route, gathering initials at each stop. All but seven of the initials were completely irrelevant, and once I learned which was which I was able to introduce a revised routing slip with only seven stops on it.

Somebody ought to tackle LC's cataloging routines with the same end in view. At present (or at any rate last time I checked) not only were there 27 possible stops a book might make; each and every book had to make all of them. There seemed to be nobody up toward the head of the line with enough authority to say, "This is just another Ellery Queen. Bypass 23 of those desks." Or perhaps the authority was there, but not the bravery required to face the indignation of the people bypassed.

(Move over, Professor Parkinson. There is now a Melcher's Law which says that in a bureaucracy every routing list will expand until it contains the maximum number of names that can be typed in a single vertical column, namely, 27.)

What we have had at LC thus far is a highly sophisticated auto-mation of the decoding of the incoming order slips, and a program (lagging) for automating the reprinting problem, but virtually no effective action on expediting the cataloging routines. The reason is not far to seek. Anyone with any skill in systems analysis is out using it to sell expensive automatic machinery, not wasting it on such trivia as getting the world's cataloging done before those who need it are forced to duplicate it themselves.

(Many, many companies are today using IBM punched cards and computers where they should be using McBee Keysort cards and knitting needles, simply because the sales commissions are higher in computers than in knitting needles. Many an uneconomic computer installation would have shown real economy if those responsible had completed the systems work but stopped just short of bringing in the computer.)

What is really needed at LC is a hard-nosed re-examination and overhaul of its cataloging procedures aimed at processing the daily work on daily newspaper schedules, instead of on what you might call "quarterly journal" schedules. If anyone, at any point, says or implies that, after all, LC is first and foremost the servant of Congress and only secondarily the servant of the nation's other libraries, then a separate agency should be set up in which top priority *can* be given to the needs of the nation's other libraries.

In any re-examination of current LC cataloging procedures, a far greater voice than ever before needs to be given to the ultimate users of the information—not, it should be emphasized, to the catalogers in the other institutions, users though they may be, but to the ultimate users, the nation's acquisitions and processing people, researchers, scholars, and readers. For far too long we have all been victimized by a kind of anachronistic perfectionism utterly out of place anywhere outside an ivory tower. There isn't one library user in a thousand who would willingly exchange one day of promptness for any of the arcane brackets with which we clutter up our catalog cards. There isn't one library user in a thousand who would willingly exchange one day of promptness for the privilege of finding the exact pagination of bibliographies within the catalog entry.

(It is sometimes argued that the notation, "Bibl.: p. 1197–1213" tells you at least that there are 17 pages of bibliography. But if this is so important, why withhold this kind of quantitative clue—why say only "Bibls."—when they are just as extensive but not contiguous?)

Nor is there one library user in a thousand who would ever notice or complain if a catalog entry credited a book with 219 pages when in fact it had xiv + 219 pages. It is, surely, useful to know whether a book is great or slight, whether it has 69 pages or 1690 pages. But it does not seem defensible to delay the world's access to anything that is worth cataloging at all just to record nuances utterly irrelevant outside rarebook rooms.

The plain fact is that speed — the kind of speed we need from LC in the area of cataloging — need not cost. It basically costs no more to catalog a book promptly than to catalog it 90 days late. In fact, it probably costs significantly less.

If LC or a separate agency established specially for the purpose is to live up to its responsibility for serving the nation's libraries as a group, it must also start paying as much attention to their convenience as to its own. The layout of LC's card order form is a shocking example of insensitivity to the needs of its library customers and their book suppliers. It is a classic case of the tail wagging the dog. (See page 27 ff. for further discussion of this problem.)

In a book on how to buy books to best advantage and, by implication, on how to buy the catalog cards needed to go with the books, I wish I could come up with some more constructive suggestions. Unhappily this is a game in which LC holds all the cards. The problem really comes down to how to get the new books into effective use in spite of LC.

Frankly, I don't believe I'd hold my breath waiting for LC to get caught up. I see no really practical alternative but to work out a standard procedure for getting a temporary author card into the public catalog and for getting the book onto the public shelves under a temporary call number. Ideally, temporary title cards and temporary subject cards should go into the public catalog as well, though this might perhaps be dispensed with if patrons were alerted to the existence of tools like *Forthcoming Books* and the *Subject Guide to Forthcoming Books* and were encouraged to use them.

Library Automation

In the fall of 1965 Harrison Bryan, librarian of the University of Sydney, Australia, paid a personal visit to most of the United States libraries which had been getting publicity about their automation programs and found next to nothing that was in any sense operational, let alone economic. His survey report, financed by a Carnegie Traveling Fellowship, was summarized in the *Library Journal* of 15 January 1967. If he were to repeat his 77-day tour today, it is unlikely that he would find many more "successes," though he would surely find more "interesting experiments," as they are generally called when they don't pan out quite as hoped.

Cynical though it may sound, one of the greatest services a librarian can render his library, be it large or small, is probably to take a stubborn, "show-me" attitude when automation is proposed. It is conceivable that the proposed automation is valid for libraries (or at least for this one) and that the would-be automaters could carry it through successfully, but on the record of recent years the chances are heavily against it. The number of people who have had *successful* experience in automating *library* procedures are few indeed.

In 1968 ALA began publishing, through its Information Science and Automation Division, a *Journal of Library Automation*. It is perhaps appropriate to note that in the first three quarterly issues only one public library project was described, and this was a project under contemplation, not one actually in operation.

135

In its annual report the Washington University School of Medicine Library reported 1967–68 as "the most frustrating year" of its planned automation of acquisitions and cataloging, despite the fact that when the year began "all the budgeted positions were filled with either librarians who had worked with computers, or computer technicians who had worked in libraries for some years." Problems included staff turnover, a change of computers, and failure of efforts to work jointly with the main library.

"Must" reading for anyone confronted with a decision about possible automation is the article, "Trial by Computer," by Basil Stuart-Stubbs in the *Library Journal* of 15 December 1967. It's fiction and it's funny, but the truth in it will make you wince. It's supposed to have happened in a college library, but the relevance to public libraries is close enough.

It is unpopular and unfashionable these days to do other than bow and scrape when automation is mentioned. Anyone who shows any hesitation about junking time-tested procedures and leaping blindfold into the world of the future is immediately compared to those who refused to rush out and buy the first horseless carriages.

It is true that someone had to buy the horseless carriages that led to improvement in the roads that led to improvement in the horseless carriages. It is open to question, however, whether each individual library is called upon to pioneer in areas where so many experiments are in progress already. Surely it is not unreasonable for a library to say: "Show us a system that is actually doing what we want done, in a situation comparable with ours, and show proof that your proposed new system is better than our present one, and then we'll talk. Don't tell us that no ready-made computer system is fully transplantable into any situation other than the one it was designed for. There are a thousand libraries with problems exactly like ours. We buy standard charging machines, standard furniture, standard typewriters. When you have one or more standard solutions to those problems tested and debugged, let us know. We can wait."

You will, of course, be told that the system being proposed to you *is* a tested system, that it is in fact being used in such-and-such a library. That may indeed be so, but under no circumstances is it safe to accept secondhand assurances of this, least of all from someone who stands to gain from getting you to jump on the automation bandwagon—whether hardware salesman, software salesman, or consultant. Check up. If the cited example is too far away to visit, bide your time. Wait until the world of the future has beaten its path a bit closer to your door.

You might, God forbid, be told of the automation at the Montclair Public Library. A brochure describing this installation was for 20 years trotted out by IBM representatives as proof that they had something for libraries. Hundreds of librarians visited Montclair to see it. Yet not even the IBM Corporation ever saw fit to duplicate the equipment that had been custom-made for this application.

When you do investigate a system represented as having been proved out, you are very likely to find: (1) that it is not in fact in actual operation, though "they" are working on it (find out how long they have been working on it, and how much longer this was than originally projected); (2) that the library tried it, but gave it up; (3) that the system is operational, but that there have been some difficulties about getting computer time when needed, and the old manual procedures (the elimination of which was the chief justification for the change) are still in use; (4) that it was an "interesting experiment" from which much was learned, but has been "temporarily" set aside; (5) that it is operational and satisfactory, but that cost comparisons between the old way and the new are unavailable; (6) that it is operational and satisfactory and productive of great savings, provided you do not count the cost of the "systems" work, the programming, the conversion, or the computer time (you may be told that the justification for not counting the cost of the computer time is that although the computer time *is being charged* to the library, this is unfair inasmuch as the early justification for the computerization was based on the idea that there was paid-for but unused time available on the computer); (7) that the system is a resounding success in every respect, except that the patrons it serves hate it.

You may also, I suppose, find a library system that has successfully solved problems exactly like yours, that has unmistakable proof of resulting gains, that is using a computer exactly like the one available to you, and that is willing to give you (or sell you) a complete set of its procedures manuals, program decks, and conversion procedures and lend you its chief operations manager for a year to train your staff and supervise the conversion of your procedures. (If you ever hear of a case of this kind, let me know.)

Far and away the best way to computerize is s-l-o-w-l-y. After all, what's the hurry? Computers are steadily coming down in price and going up in versatility. There may even come a time when the supply of competent programmers begins to catch up to the demand. (If you think it is hard to find and attract qualified librarians, wait until you start looking for computer personnel in a field where someone with six months' experience is considered an old hand and where standards of accreditation are unknown.)

In the world of business the decision to explore automation is often based on competitive considerations. The feeling is that it might be risky to let a competitor get too far ahead. A public library should presumably be able to resist this kind of pressure. You are not in competition with other public libraries, and if other libraries choose to blaze the trail, you can reasonably assume that you will have easy access to what they learn.

Eventually, perhaps, it will even be possible to get pretested "software," instead of being on your own from the time they wheel in the hardware. You may never before have bought any device that did not come with some sort of guarantee that it would do the work you bought it to do. Not so with computers. If your programs don't work in the machine you rented, that's your problem. One library wholesaler installed precisely what IBM recommended, only to find that it was woefully inadequate, at which the IBM salesman cheerfully conceded his mistake and proposed to correct it by bringing in three times the equipment at three times the rental.

When a school publication found its new computer installation completely inadequate to process its September subscription load, the computer company's "experts" apologized and said, "Evidently we failed to note that a school publication must process more subscriptions in September than in any other month."

Another possible reason for moving slowly is to allow time for examining your library's own automation needs in the context of county or state needs. You ought to be getting your feet wet, but it could be wise to defer any big plunge until you can feel sure it wouldn't lock you out of desirable cooperative ventures a few years ahead or perhaps deprive you of a chance to share heavy conversion costs with others.

You may well be told: "Gradual conversion is piecemeal conversion. Why computerize the paying of people and not the paying of vendors? Why computerize your purchasing and paying but not your cataloging? And if the cataloging, why not take the next logical step and abolish your card catalogs and substitute printed book catalogs? And if you computerize your catalog, why not plan for mechanized searching of the catalog? And while you are at it, what about moving farther into automatic ordering plans to save the time of the book selectors for the more difficult buying decisions?"

It can be further argued against gradual conversion that massive changes are more likely to succeed than gradual changes. Where backsliding is possible, backsliding must be expected. Most people can do things better at first by old familiar methods than by new and unfamiliar methods; witness the resistance of hunt-and-peck typists to learning touch typing.

Finally, gradual conversion is theoretically more costly than all-at-once conversion. False paths are taken. Machine operations require parallel payrolls and duplicate housing. Considering that there is going to be staff unhappiness in any case, isn't it better to get it over with as fast as possible?

But there is also a strong case for gradualism. It gives the staff time to adjust to the new technology, and it can be quite a wrench to accept the idea that invisible magnetic dots on a reel of magtape are going to *replace* a trusty card file. The library also needs time to develop inside expertise. Why should we assume that a still-wet-behind-the-ears graduate of some crash course in computers should be able to pick up what he needs to know about library science any more readily than a librarian should be able to pick up what he or she needs to know about computer science?

And while gradualism may lead to false starts, at least it keeps the mistakes *small*. No one ever set up a large plan, either, who didn't later have some second thoughts on how he should have done it.

Easing into automation is probably also best in terms of staff relations. No matter how many pronouncements are made about how no one will lose his job, staff members are going to go right on believing that no computerization plan will ever be considered successful unless the computer displaces enough other salaries to cover its own personnel and rental. Management may be convinced that normal staff turnover will take care of this, but this is cold comfort for those staff members who were not planning to leave but who see their present work being taken over by the computer. To relieve the fear of the unknown, they need time to get some idea of what they might be doing after retraining.

One of the commonest arguments in favor of automation is that it will "save manpower." But it is worth asking whether the project under consideration will save the kind of manpower you most want to save. Are your recruitment problems most acute at the professional level, and the projected staff savings all at the lowest clerical level?

Automation in the library can take many forms, ranging from simple bookkeeping to full integration of acquisitions, cataloging, serials control, circulation control, and information retrieval. Hardly anybody is in very deep as yet, but some big dreams are being dreamt. As might be expected, the problems of automating a payroll or a system for encumbering and paying, being of universal applicability, have had a good deal more study than the problems of automating a library catalog.

One of the most difficult aspects of any automation program is in deciding which "expert" to rely on. It is extremely difficult for the layman to distinguish between degrees of expertise. In this field, more than in most, a little knowledge is a dangerous thing. The tip-off to superficiality of knowledge is usually an insistence that anything is possible, that technologies proved by the banks, or the airlines, or the stock market are all at the service of your library.

Experts fall into several types. There is the "cloud nine" type, who has never stopped to consider how many transactions per minute it takes to validate the techniques used by the banks, airlines, or Wall Street; who has never priced the rental costs of coaxial cable (he doesn't even know that ordinary phone lines won't carry TV screen images); who hasn't grasped the important distinctions between tape storage, disc storage, and core storage. He knows you *can* do anything by computer, but he hasn't stopped to ask whether anyone in his right mind would want to.

Then there is the "programmer" who has undeniably been earning a living at his trade, but who knows about as much of systems design as a radio assembly-line worker knows of electronics. He may have been translating from people-language into computer-language without ever even wondering whether the instructions made sense in terms of the goals.

Then there is the computer-oriented systems analyst. If he's any good, he will be a compulsive problem-solver and may well spend highly paid time solving problems you don't even want solved, e.g., how to devise computer routines to do small-volume chores that could be done quicker by hand. If he's an inspired problem-solver, this may or may not go hand in hand with the knack of keeping costs in mind. His personal motivations also warrant consideration; he wouldn't be human if he didn't put personal income or future prospects ahead of your goals. If you got him by outbidding someone else for his services, you may well lose him by the same route.

No decision to automate should ever be taken except in the context of an overall systems analysis made by someone who *is not necessarily committed* to any particular approach. This can be important. First, you don't want to set up an automated way of doing what you don't want done anyway, and as a general rule, the automaters will give you what you say you want rather than question it. Second, you don't want to prejudice the answers. Perhaps you should *not* get a computer just yet, so you don't want a computer-happy consultant who never even considers anything else.

All too often, discussion of computerization *starts* with the observation that the library could get some time on a computer located elsewhere, but imperceptibly moves into consideration of programs that would require the full time of an inside computer, or at least access to an entirely different kind of outside computer. The cost of computer time, either way, bears review.

The rental on a typical small computer tends to start at about $3,000 a month, including fairly minimal accessories, and can run up to $10,000 a month with surprising ease, if any considerable amount of versatility is demanded. Sharing a computer with other agencies can, of course, result in a sharing of these costs; time shared equitably on a comparatively modest computer often works out to about $25 an hour, which is not as far below the rates of commercial service bureaus as at first appears when you remember that you pay for your own mistakes when you pay "inside" rates.

A good question to keep sharply in mind is whether the computer applications under discussion would require communication with the computer *during the hours the library is open.* If so, then you are probably going to need an in-house computer all your own. If not, then time on an outside computer might suffice.

No discussion of computerization ever goes very far without touching on prospects involving "random access," i.e., the capacity to interrogate the computer at any time and get an immediate answer. An attractive possibility, for example, is querying the computer on every charge-out to find out whether this particular borrower is in arrears. This is possible. But this alone could tie up a small computer, or make substantial demands on a large one, and invoke rental costs of several thousand dollars a month. Is it worth it?

Another attractive possibility is having in random-access computer memory the entire information in the card catalog, plus information about books on order. In theory this data store could be interrogated at will from any desired number of locations, determining instantly whether a desired title is in the system or on order, where located, and whether on loan. However, the cost of such a system — even for a library with only 100,000 titles — could well run to $15,000 a month or more, not counting some very impressive start-up and conversion costs. (One of the most sobering moments in exploring computerization ideas is when you find out what the *telephone company* will charge for hooking in remote terminals, since rental of

4. Is there a class of book in our library which is always in circulation and never on the shelf? Should we buy more duplicate copies of these, so that those patrons who browse and select from what they find will not be deprived of the chance to see occasionally on the shelves the books that the reserve borrowers are queueing up for?

5. Is there a class of book in our library which never circulates, though purchased with circulation in mind?

6. Do we have a practical means of informing ourselves about these "never-in" or "never-out" titles for whatever the information might teach us about how to improve our selection procedures? If not, should we seek such a capability in any new approach to circulation control?

7. Do we know how many people use our various departments except as circulation figures reveal it? Should we know this, or at least spot-check it regularly in case some reallocation of space or staff should seem indicated to give the greatest service to the greatest number?

8. What, precisely, are the reasons for making and filing each piece of paper we handle? Do we know the cost of maintaining each file? The number of times it is used? The cost per use? Does this cost seem justified in every case? Of all the files we keep, which is the one that would be least missed if not kept? (And are all our files up to date? If not, is this perhaps presumptive evidence that the ones not being kept up are not really vital?)

9. Are we perhaps taking certain security measures on a 100-percent basis when spot checking might suffice? For example, could we afford to pay on receipt of invoice, without awaiting positive verification of receipt of books, in reliance on the good faith and ultimate accountability of our vendors?

10. What percentage of our income goes for books? Why is this figure what it is? (Statistics drawn from the successive editions of the *American Library Directory* show that the average percent of public library funds going for books has been moving quite steadily upward, but ranges from 10 percent to 25 percent. British practice puts the range a bit higher.)

A major goal of computerizing ordering procedures seems often to be a foolproof way of encumbering funds. Not all libraries, however, consider it *important* to encumber funds on an item-by-item basis. Some simply ask each branch or department to stay roughly within assigned budgetary limits and trust them to do so. After all, how far overboard could they go? (It is sometimes also possible to put the burden for not going beyond prescribed limits on the vendor.)

There are some good reasons to study the potentials of automation. There are also some poor reasons, e.g., that there is idle time on a computer housed elsewhere; that some computer-happy systems man elsewhere in the city wants a computer and wants you to help him justify it; that someone, somewhere, is being called unprogressive and wants to prove he isn't; that the work of a certain department is in a mess and "automation" is the first answer that comes to mind.

Evaluations of the advantages of computerization commonly cheat a little. Projected costs, based on the assumption that everything has been foreseen and that nothing will go wrong, are compared with actual past costs which included the unforeseen. Projected costs usually assume total abolition of former files and procedures; in an actual case, a five-part form was to be replaced by a one-part form, but the five-part form survived *also*. Projected costs often assume certain sacrifices, e.g., radical abridgment of the information on the catalog card, but without exploration of what such abridgment might save under existing procedures.

Projected advantages place great stress on new capabilities for data analysis, whether or not these alone would seem worth a high price. The Montclair Public Library's punched-card circulation system had been highly touted as permitting all kinds of analysis; yet after one round of experimentation with this novel but not particularly instructive kind of analysis, the capability was not even used again for 20 years.

In the computer field, where IBM has the lion's share of the overall business, it nevertheless pays to remember that RCA and Honeywell and NCR and GE and Control Data are all competing and should definitely be allowed to make proposals or bid on your specs. RCA won the contract to automate the card division of the Library of Congress. Many publishers use Honeywell equipment, and at least one changed over from IBM to Honeywell. It is not even inevitable that a library should select the same kind of equipment used elsewhere in its system. Two computers from the same manufacturer are not necessarily compatible with each other, and two computers from different manufacturers are not necessarily *in*compatible with each other.

Is there a computer in your library's future? Undoubtedly. But it is a pity that the words "automation" and "computer" are so often used as if they were synonymous both with each other and with "forward-looking." So much emphasis on the "machine" tends to obscure the fact that machines are only one tool of effective management. In a great many situations a rethinking of procedures that have really had no recent review may well produce fairly important breakthroughs *without* introduction of any hardware. Not only the march of invention, but also changes in salary levels, goals, and attitudes suggest that all procedures of long standing should be required to rejustify themselves from time to time. It is quite literally true that many an unsuccessful computer conversion might well have shown substantial gains, if only those responsible had stopped just short of actually bringing in the computer.

How to Buy Serials to Best Advantage

Nowhere in library acquisition practice is the bid system more of a handicap than in ordering serials, and those libraries still committed to the bid process are in real difficulty. The more responsible subscription agents are simply declining to bid. Almost without exception college and university libraries no longer require bid-letting and, according to Hensel and Veillette (in *Purchasing Library Materials in Public and School Libraries*),75 percent of public libraries and 63 percent of school libraries no longer require it. Those librarians who are still trying to work under a bid system hate it with a passion equaled only by that of the more conscientious subscription agents.

The heart of the problem lies in the fact that a subscription is an ongoing thing. By rights the subscription agent should be held responsible not only for placing or renewing subscriptions but also for follow-through: investigating lapses, claiming missing issues, taking advantage of two-year and three-year offers, seeing that new subscriptions scheduled to start next January *do* start next January, and so on. Annual changes of agent make this impossible. In the complex area of subscriptions, a change of agents is a catastrophe to be avoided at almost any cost, not invited on an annual basis.

Speaking at the ALA Pre-Conference on Acquisitions in Atlantic City in July 1969, William H. Huff, Serials Librarian at the University of Illinois Libraries in Urbana, said:

147

The bid system is an irritant for both agents and most librarians. Perhaps it can be tolerated by small city libraries and by limited special libraries where record control may not be as complex, or where a change from one dealer to another may not be as disastrous or disrupting as in large operations. However, it seems a bit archaic for libraries pushing 1,000 subscriptions or more to be saddled with this 19th-century purchasing mechanism.

Happily the bid system is losing ground. Among the 46 research and academic libraries I questioned, only one used the bid system for periodical subscriptions, and this only because compelled by law. Such an on-again, off-again way of doing business does not foster the development of warm, sincere, or even satisfactory relationships between library and agent.

The few dollars which may sway the balance in the mind of the purchasing office or the administration as to who will be awarded the contract does not as a rule compensate for the library's added internal operational expenses. Fortunately the trend is away from the bid system. Unless you have proven to yourself that you are benefiting from the bid system, it is time to take a firm stand, as serials librarians, and fight the system. There are a lot of us who will support you.

Frank F. Clasquin of the F. W. Faxon Company writes:

Responsible agencies cannot enter discount bids and in some cases find it necessary to add a service charge. The library or its procurement authority should, therefore, prudently review the matter of annual bid requests on their periodical needs, questioning why this method of renewal action is being followed. Only the librarian can evaluate the quality of service rendered by the agency and should be requested to assist the purchasing authority in the selection of a responsible agency.

S. L. Smith of the Moore-Cottrell Subscription Agencies writes:

Cost alone should not be the determining factor. We believe that schools and libraries should consider placing subscriptions for longer terms without bids or on a standing-order basis to save money, at the same time helping vendors render the type of service rightfully demanded and expected.

The primary recommendation in the Hensel and Veillette study is, "Library materials, including periodicals, should be exempt from the normal bid requirement of purchasing agencies."

The question may be asked whether the practice of placing subscription contracts by bid has always been undesirable or whether this is something new. To a certain extent it has always been undesirable, and many libraries have never done it. However, there are also new factors. More periodicals are being published. Libraries which once took 100 may now take 1,000. The new periodicals often give little or no discount to the agents. There has been a sharp trend away from "net paid" circulation and in the direction of "controlled free" circulation.

Between the negotiation of any contract and its implementation it is far more likely than formerly that the publishers will have raised their prices or reduced their discount to agents. There are other problems that make it difficult for an agent to enter a responsible bid. There is the problem of the new publication which suspends after a few months but does not refund; no agent can reasonably be expected to make good on defaults that are not his. An agent can reasonably be expected to try for a refund on serials discontinued by the publisher or canceled by the subscriber, and he can *try* for missing back issues, but he cannot do more.

There is also the little matter of the *cost* of entering a bid. Quoting on library subscription needs is expensive and takes time because it must be done with care; a bidder who makes a blind stab without close study of your library's wants and idiosyncrasies can take a real beating. The library which is required to seek bids is often expected to get at least three. Obviously two of the bidders will have nothing to show for their pains. None are going to be happy if they seem to be cast in the role of "always a bridesmaid, never a bride."

Sometimes it seems to a library laboring under some kind of low-bid tyranny as if its problems would be solved if it were just free to weigh factors other than price in evaluating the bids. But if a library wins this point, so that it is saying in effect, "All right, we'll invite bids if we must, but it'll be surprising if we change suppliers because we couldn't afford to give the contract to anybody but good old so-and-so; it would be too much agony during the changeover," this library is going to find "other bidders" becoming pretty scarce. It becomes quickly apparent that no good can come from any compromise between the formal bid-letting procedure and the informal negotiation of a contract.

If one concedes the force of the arguments in favor of picking one subscription agent and sticking with him year after year, the problem then is how to keep him from overcharging. This is not perhaps as serious a problem as might first appear, because the library still retains a good 90 percent of its bargaining power in that 90 percent of the face value of the contract doesn't go *to* the agent, it goes *through* the agent to the periodical publishers. The real bid-letting, the real comparison shopping, continues because it takes place on another level, namely the selection level.

The important prices, the publishers' prices, are quite beyond the control of either agent or library, but the library can still pay or refuse to pay. It can and will weigh *Forbes* against *Dun's,* or *Modern Photography* against *Popular Photography,* to determine which seems best in price, scope, indexing, and so on.

The question of whether the agent takes a markup of 10 percent on the money he handles, or perhaps 12 percent, is not a matter of no concern, but it is distinctly secondary to making sure that full value is received for the rest of the money. Favoring the agent willing to work on 10 percent over another agent asking 12 percent, on that ground alone, is a bit like buying lunches or dentistry on price alone. There is all too strong a possibility that if you pay less, you won't like what you get.

Of course, there must still be some means of keeping a supplier's charges in line, and incidentally of making certain that he not only delivers value for value received, but also that no one inside or outside the library could reasonably suspect otherwise. That means staying open-minded about alternatives, comparing notes with other libraries on their experience with other suppliers, and perhaps splitting off a bit of business for a newcomer, to give him a chance to show what he might do.

The idea that an agent should be able to offer any discount at all stems from the fact that some of the most widely circulated consumer magazines do commonly undercut their own subscription "list" prices and encourage agents to do likewise. A publication which relies chiefly on advertising for its income may not expect much net revenue from subscriptions. There is a provision in the U.S. Post Office Regulations regarding second-class mail that to be eligible for these low postal rates (which in 1970 started at 3.4 cents a pound on editorial matter), a publication must have bona fide *paying* subscribers, paying not less than one-half the published subscription price. This is why you often get "half-price introductory offers" but never any deeper cut, though a publisher may well spend whatever money you do send him on the promotion that persuaded you to do it. It is not uncommon in consumer periodical publishing to budget as if there would be *no* net revenue from subscriptions—discounts would take half and promotion the other half.

Once you get past the mass-circulation magazines, however, the situation changes drastically. Some of the trade publications go to a "controlled free" basis of circulation, under which *they* decide whom they want for subscribers (or rather whom their advertisers want to reach), to whom they mail free. It increases their postage somewhat (to 15 cents a pound or fraction thereof) but it relieves them of the problem of having to cajole the subscribers into sending in even half of list price. Magazines with less advertising, on the other hand — professional, scholarly, technical, and scientific journals — are more dependent on subscription revenues and far less disposed to make cut-price offers. Some give discounts to agents, but usually try to hold them to a minimum to discourage the agents from undercutting the publisher's own price.

Thus agents can still quote discounts to librarians with very simple wants (though perhaps no more than these same librarians could get at home as individuals if they watched the special offers), but they are increasingly unable to make any kind of discount showing on the longer lists of larger libraries.

It may be asked whether a library would be well advised to use an agent if the agent were unable to offer any overall cash saving as against placing orders direct with the publisher. Many librarians seem satisfied that an agent's services are worth paying for, even if they result in no extra discounts beyond what the library could get for itself by dealing direct. The difference between sending one order and one payment to one agent and sending 1,000 subscriptions and 1,000 payments to 1,000 publishers can easily come to several thousand dollars in inside clerical costs.

According to one experienced agent, the cost of the average journal is now $16, and the cost of servicing library subscriptions runs about 10–12 percent of the price. If these two estimates are divided one into the other, we are perhaps being told that an agent's service charge for handling one $16 subscription carrying no publisher discount to him might have to be from $1.60 to $1.92.

Every library must make its own determination of the cost of placing 1,000 orders with 1,000 publishers as against placing one order with one agent. It is unlikely that such a cost could be less than $2 per order, which on 1,000 orders would hardly cover one clerk one day a week with related overheads and fringe benefits. In most situations this cost will more likely run from $5 to $10; one must remember that both library personnel and business office personnel will be involved, and that the correspondence will inevitably go well beyond the one order/one bill/one payment minimum. (In many organizations it costs a good $5 just to write a check.)

However, *if* it could be ascertained, or perhaps just stipulated for

151

the sake of the argument, that it would cost $4 per directly placed subscription above the cost of dealing through an agent, and *if* the agent were asking a fee figured at cost plus 12 percent (and averaging $2 per subscription), then clearly there would be a good case for using the agent for any subscription priced up to $40 a year, and perhaps a good case for going direct to the publisher on (say) a $200 subscription, on which an agent's 12 percent would come to $24. It might also be worth going direct to the publisher on any multiple subscriptions *totaling* more than $40 or $50, e.g., five subscriptions at $10 each.

On the other hand, to avoid the dual procedure, it might be possible to work out some compromise with the agent under which he would avoid creating this incentive to buy around him. A flat $2.50 *per line item* might be one answer, although some increment on the more costly journals might be in order, inasmuch as there are service costs related to cost. For example, the agent who lays out $200 today for a single costly journal and is reimbursed by the library three months later might incur an extra expense of $6 in interest on bank loans at current rates. And an honest mistake might be more costly to rectify. (As mentioned elsewhere, surely the best answer to the burden of payments unreasonably delayed would be a simple interest charge on any balance unpaid past 30 days.) A service charge of some kind becomes inevitable when agents get no discount themselves, when the discount is inadequate to cover their costs, or when they are asked to obtain "controlled free" publications.

An educational campaign is very much needed to persuade the publishers of some kinds of journals of the value *to them* (and to their advertisers) of library subscriptions. Some take the line that since they are *giving* subscriptions to all the professionals of interest to their advertisers, none of these professionals would be likely to seek a copy in the library, and valuable copies can't be wasted. Some of these publishers honor selected requests, but also reserve the right to decline. It is, of course, extremely frustrating to any librarian to be told that a journal demonstrably in demand by library patrons is not (in the judgment of the publisher) likely to enjoy such demand. Occasionally special pleading will break down an initial refusal, though perhaps only for a time.

Perhaps there should be some better and more businesslike answer. Perhaps the special postage rates extended to controlled free publications should be conditioned upon publisher cooperation with publicly supported libraries, at least to the extent of supplying any library willing to pay the cost of paper, printing, and postage. To prevent the setting of unreasonable rates, these could be stipulated as not to exceed (say) five times the cost of the postage. Granted that libraries paid enough to cover paper and printing and postage, library circulation would probably be welcomed by the advertisers.

Perhaps enough has been said about the problems that subscription agents have with librarians. It is time to say a bit about the problems that librarians have with subscription agents. Some clearly relate to the problems of devising and debugging computer procedures. Presumably no agent intentionally continues to refer to a publication by a long superseded title, or attempts to place a renewal with a now-defunct publication, but this is exactly the kind of thing that can happen during a computer conversion. Presumably time and patience are the only cures for such problems. The winners in the race for computerization may be those who do it last and learn from the mistakes of others.

By far the most numerous complaints undoubtedly go back to problems of *publisher* inefficiency or indifference, quite beyond the control of any agent. After all, the publishers, too, have, many of them, been computerizing, with the usual results. In the words of Joseph D. O'Shaughnessy of Neodata Services in New York:

> When you complain, give us full data, including every character on the address label, no matter how cryptic. When a computer starts abusing you, it's no good retorting "You stupid jerk . . ." unless you can also feed its own language right back to it.

Agents tend to get the blame even when it is the publisher who doesn't answer his mail, won't start a subscription in the middle of *his* year, takes three months to get the issues flowing, refuses to cancel or refund, sends renewal notices that aren't called for, and declines to give the agent enough commission to operate on.

Entirely apart from the routine static resulting from computer conversions and breakdowns, human error, and staff changes and vacancies, one of the biggest problems with publishers is that servicing library subscribers is anything but uppermost on their list of priorities. Some publishers are primarily oriented to a trade or industry, to a membership, or to a profession. Some don't want to be bothered with back-dated subscriptions. Some don't want to start new subscriptions until the end of *their* year. Some don't acknowledge subscriptions or respond to inquiries about them, yet will suddenly start sending issues months after a would-be subscriber has written them off.

Unless a publisher is heavily dependent on libraries for his subscription revenue, he often couldn't care less if all libraries dropped dead. From where he sits, libraries are just trouble. They order in May, wanting service from January. If he sends them the January-to-May back issues and starts new issues with June, it develops they meant *next* January. He has no provision for entering a subscription that does not start immediately, but he sets up a "bring-up" file in which he hopes he will remember to look come next November, to activate this subscription. The libraries don't send cash with order like ordinary subscribers, but seem to expect to be billed. When he bills them, they come back with a demand that he bill them on *their* bill forms, notarized, in quintuplicate. He renders such a bill, but months pass without payment. Ultimately he suspends the subscription and forgets the whole thing. *Then* they pay, and a new clerk has to write to try to find out what they are trying to pay *for*. They are indignant over the missed issues and feel he should have known that their business office always pays eventually. Six to 18 months after date of issue, they write to say that their binding runs are incomplete, and will he please supply the missing issues.

Libraries are perhaps 2 percent of the publisher's subscribers and cause 52 percent of the headaches in his subscription department. To cap the climax, they suggest, apparently in dead seriousness, that the publisher redesign his cover and contents page to conform to some standard of no possible interest to the other 98 percent of his subscribers, as if he didn't have enough problems of his own with printing requirements, postal requirements, point-of-sale requirements, editorial deadlines, and a host of other pressures.

The "missing-issue" problem is acute. Publishers feel imposed on if you wait until next year to claim issues missing from this year's binding set and suspect (probably rightly in most cases) that the issues went astray *after* you received them, not before. From your point of view, you need the missing issues no matter who lost them, and you can't claim them before you know they are missing.

It is inevitable, too, that publishers will occasionally underprint and run out of copies of an issue. There probably ought to be a central Missing Issues Bureau. You'd claim from the publisher on a double postcard. The return half would have two places to check, either (1) "Yes, sending" or (2) "Sorry, no longer available, feel free to Xerox." You'd then send to the MIB for a Xerox replacement. Since I think there is probably a pattern to the issues we lose, the MIB might even be able to reprint in dozens, scores, or hundreds those issues particularly susceptible to mysterious disappearance or underprinted by the publisher.

When I was at Bowker I used to get a lot of letters about serials problems, or sometimes carbon copies of letters to others, and I used to keep a file of what seemed like interesting observations or suggestions. Some of these follow. Unfortunately, I've mislaid the originals and thus can't give credit where credit is due:

> Our gripes are with publishers, not with agents. We feel we are at the mercy of issuing bodies. We can always change agents, but not a publisher.

> You can't *expect* to get businesslike answers out of un-businesslike people, and let's face it, the typical journal publisher isn't a "publisher" at all; he's a society, or a trade association, or a scholar—even a library.

> Maybe we shouldn't even try to work through the agents on claims for missing issues. After all, what can they do but forward the requests? We might as well claim direct. Agencies can be invaluable on organizing common terminations, spotting worthwhile three-year offers, helping us stay within budget limits, and breaking down our big payments into hundreds of smaller ones. But we don't need them on claims and probably shouldn't burden them.

> If you can't take advantage of three-year offers—well, just *figure out* a way because it *pays*. Even when they don't push them, a good two-thirds of the publishers will accept them, and even when the three-year rate is three times the one-year rate, you save the paper work and get protection against price increases. And in many cases the savings are well worthwhile.

> About the time a subscription agent finally gets his computer debugged, he'll have a new problem, namely, with our computer. And if we ever *all* get our computers under control, then the agents can *really* worry, because we'll be able to punish unsatisfactory performance by simply flipping a switch.

> Many libraries use several overseas agents. Why not use two or three domestic agents also? In other words, invite bids but divide the load between the best two or three instead of giving it all to one? It would give you a better chance to compare performance.

> It would be *nice* if all journals would carry a standard serial identity number in a standard place but forget it unless you can make it a condition of postal privileges. Bill Huff [of the University of Illinois Libraries in Urbana] says he probed this and couldn't even get the library periodicals to agree.

I am indebted to Frank F. Clasquin, vice-president of the F. W. Faxon Company, for the following summary of services which a library can expect from a responsible subscription agency (drawn from his article in the Spring 1965 *Sci-Tech News*):

1. Flexibility of subscription terms with advice on how the library's budgeted funds can be used to purchase the maximum number of periodicals consistent with its purchasing policies or legal limitations. Options open to the library are:

a. Place all subscriptions for a one-year period.

b. Place two-year subscriptions whenever they are available at reduced rates.

c. Place three-year subscriptions whenever they are available at reduced rates.

d. Where reduced rates are not available, place three-year subscriptions anyway, thus taking advantage of the savings in time and paper work that come with placing one order instead of three.

e. Place three-year subscriptions on all titles but rotate them so that one-third of the list comes up for renewal each year, thus maintaining approximately the same invoice balance from year to year.

(NOTE: To give some idea of the savings to be gained from three-year subscriptions, a recent analysis of some 23,000 titles showed that although 65 percent of the publishers offered three-year rates, only 45 percent offered actual reductions in price, the remainder simply quoting multiples of the annual rate.)

2. Updating, based on list of deletions and additions supplied by the library. Library should not have to supply a complete list of titles annually. The agency can work from the list of additions and deletions, incorporating them into the previous year's list, and the final invoice reflecting these changes can serve as the library's record.

3. Detailed invoice, showing such information as:

a. The subscription period or volume number for which the library is charged and the publisher paid.

b. Any special addresses or individual names to which the library has requested that selected titles be mailed.

c. Explanation, if a title has not been charged on the invoice for the current period (publication discontinued, title must be ordered directly from the publisher, publisher is slow, etc.)

d. Identification of those titles which are non-cancellable, foreign, annuals, calendar year only, one year only, volume year only.

4. Common expiration date.

5. Cancellation of unwanted subscriptions in accordance with publishers' restrictions and refunding of unexpired portions.

6. Automatic ordering of annuals, yearbooks, regular or irregular proceedings or transactions published by learned societies and institutions, etc., generally handled on a "bill as published" basis.

7. Ordering of back numbers.

8. Ordering of sample copies for examination by the library.

9. Constantly up-dated records, so that expiration dates are correct and publisher, library, and agency records are in accord.

10. Active attempt to retrieve refunds from discontinued publications.

11. Maintenance of records which will promptly explain fulfillment delays or "slow" publications.

12. Handling of foreign periodicals through responsible sources.

13. Placement of memberships in learned societies where permitted.

14. Handling of the detailed correspondence with publishers as questions arise which could cause service irregularities.

15. Maintenance of an order and payment detail record for each title where current and previous payments can be traced. With such a record, claims from publishers can be settled promptly and accurately. Photo copies of the original order and cancelled checks are the most positive proof and should be instantly available when needed.

16. Prompt handling of claims to maximize the possibility of getting missing issues before publishers' stocks are depleted. A claim procedure which reduces correspondence to a minimum and yet insures positive action is extremely important.

17. Adjustment of duplicate receipt errors.

18. Advising publishers of the library's change-of-address when necessary.

19. Entering of new or additional subscriptions throughout the year to achieve a common expiration month.

20. Proving and handling of added charges from publishers for additional volumes or other charges resulting from a change in publisher policy.

21. Annual catalog, supplied without charge, listing all current periodicals and giving price, frequency, volume, index information, etc.

How to Buy Reprints

Must reprints be as expensive as they are? What can be done to discourage premature publication announcements, leading to premature commitment of funds? What can be done to discourage reprinters who change titles, omit references to series, create series out of unrelated volumes, and have unacceptably low standards of workmanship or scholarship? Isn't there any way to avoid the waste inherent in having two or more reprinters reviving the same title at the same time?

Frankly, I can see no way to dampen the enthusiasm of the less responsible reprinters except to stop buying their wares. If a reprint is overpriced and shoddy, *must* you buy it? Couldn't you perhaps just do without, at least until the work is actually called for? True, it might cost more then, or be no longer obtainable, but there is always microfilm or Xerox. Sometimes, too, the mere announcement of a reprint makes it worthwhile to try again in the out-of-print market.

Reprinters can (and will) reprint anything that enough libraries will buy. Where enough research libraries are buying everything in their fields, reprinters have a ready-made market for just about anything they can produce. Furthermore, reprinting is economically possible today at almost any level from the single-copy Xeroxed reprint on up. If there were even 25 major libraries ready, willing, and able to buy a reprint of every volume in the *National Union Catalog*, I daresay those reprints could and would be made.

The reprinter who timidly orders an edition of 500, though far from sure he can sell even 400, may well price for a get-out at a sale of 300. If he nevertheless sells 500, he can make a thumping big profit. With benefit of hindsight as to the size of the sales potential, a great many of the reprints of recent years could well have been priced lower.

What is less clear is whether the publisher *would* have priced lower even if he had known he could sell more. Publishers are under no obligation to keep their profits "reasonable"; in fact, copyright is a sort of legal license to price, not just for an adequate profit, but for a maximum profit.

If a publisher's experience tells him that 300 or 400 research libraries will buy a certain reprint whether he prices it high or low, why should he price low? In the field of the scholarly reprint, a lower price may not increase the sales enough to matter.

Other complaints about reprinters tend to come in contradictory pairs. I have one letter in my files complaining because they sometimes reprint one or two titles in a series but not the whole series. I have another letter complaining because they *will* reprint a whole series, even though there are only a few worthwhile items in it.

It is said they don't reprint enough, and that they reprint too much. It is said that a reprint represents a golden opportunity to enlarge a type size that was originally too small. *And* it is said that a reprint should faithfully follow every detail of the original, type size and all.

It is said that a reprinter should secure authorization for reprinting even material that is out of copyright and pay at least a nominal royalty. *And* it is said that this is absurd, that the law which provided the initial protection also provided and intended that the work should ultimately fall into the public domain.

My own feeling is that the really big libraries, the ones that make the reprints possible, owe it to themselves to step into the reprint situation and make their buying power count. To that end, I would like to throw out the following idea for study and possible action. I believe it would benefit libraries and reprinters alike by preventing duplication, helping evaluate sales potential, setting standards for titling, and so on.

The basic idea would be to set up, perhaps under the Association of Research Libraries, perhaps independently, a sort of Reprint Registration Bureau, whose basic function would be to "license" proposed reprints, i.e., to say in effect to the first applicant who satisfied its criteria, "Okay, you may advertise that this reprint has our approval, and you may count on it that we won't give similar approval to any other reprinter, provided you proceed on the schedule indicated." Such licensing would be binding on no one, but could be conclusively effective if even a few research libraries made it a policy not to buy reprints that lacked this approval.

You are probably thinking, "Melcher's really off the deep end on this one," but hear me out. I think there might be a way around some of the difficulties you are thinking of.

You ask, "Would the Justice Department consider this restraint of trade?" I don't know, but we could find out. With the provisions and restrictions I have in mind, I honestly don't think it would restrain anything but abuses and might reasonably be looked upon as a form of cooperative buying, aimed simply at enabling tax-supported agencies to make the taxpayers' money go farther. If it could do this and have the support of the reprinters as well, who could oppose it? As I see the plan, it would work as follows:

Anyone proposing to reprint an out-of-print title, whether in or out of copyright, would apply to the Reprint Registration Bureau for its green light. In the event that the applicant was the original copyright owner or acting under license from the copyright owner, the issuance of the certificate would be a formality, a foregone conclusion.

In the event that the work was in the public domain, the RRB would nevertheless grant the requested certificate of convenience — like the Good Housekeeping Seal of Approval — if the following conditions were met: (1) if to its knowledge no one else was planning such a reprint; and (2) if the application was accompanied by a check for 2 percent of the anticipated gross sales (price × printing).

It would be understood that if the work did not appear by the date proposed in the application, the certification would become invalid and the payment would be forfeited. Extensions could be granted only by mutual consent.

The RRB would not have the power to withhold its certification if the above conditions were met, even if it felt the proposed pricing was excessive, but it would be entitled to give its reasons for feeling that there would be advantage to all in a larger printing and a lower price. The reprinter would not be obliged to seek the certification, and he would be entirely free to go ahead with his plans even without it.

The first reprinter to seek and get the certification would be virtually assured of a clear field, even on a book in the public domain. He would thus be encouraged to plan for a larger printing at a lower cost. He would be reluctant, however, to announce a publication date he did not really think he could meet, since this could mean putting

161

up another deposit to get the certification renewed—or possible loss through default to another reprinter. (The second man to apply could perhaps be given the nod if the first defaulted.) The publication dates given in *Reprints in Progress* would thus become more meaningful, and libraries would be less burdened by the need to reallocate encumbered funds where a book ordered in good faith was not delivered within the permitted time span.

The issuance of the certification could be dependent on a full bibliographical check on the accuracy of the proposed title and title page. The 2-percent levy would be used to cover the operating expenses of the RRB, including market studies aimed at helping the reprinters to gauge the market potential for a title. Of course, a 1-percent levy might suffice, or a 2-percent levy might be inadequate, but I think 2 percent should suffice, and it would have the merit of not being so big as to be burdensome, or so small as to leave reprinters in the position of not caring whether they forfeited it.

Naturally, the biggest problems would be in the first year of the program, dealing with what's now in press, etc. I can see plenty of problems, but perhaps none would be insuperable.

It might be desirable to consider all initial applications received within (say) 90 days of each other as having been received simultaneously, and to consider later applications as simultaneous if received within 30 days of each other. In any case, a procedure would be needed to decide between simultaneous applications. Other things being equal, perhaps this kind of choice could be made on the basis of proposed publication date, price, special features, or some combination of them.

I would not like to leave too much discretion to the RRB staff, lest it open them to accusations of favoritism. Perhaps some scale could be worked out under which points were awarded for various features, and the nod went to the reprinter whose application rolled up the most points. For example, application date: 1 point for each week ahead of second application, up to five weeks; publication date: 1 point per month ahead of the other fellow; price: 1 point for each 5 percent below the other fellow; index added if originally lacking: 5 points; permanent paper: 5 points; hard binding: 5 points; concomitant commitment to reprint other volumes in same series: 5 points per other volume.

The "added index" feature could be difficult to make meaningful, but as between "simultaneous" applications, the one proposing to add a needed index certainly deserves to have an edge. The effect of such an evaluation scale would be to make permanent paper and hard binding mandatory, and to make the reprinters remember that price *might* matter.

If I were a reprinter I would see one big flaw in the above procedure as it stands, namely, the possibility that I would apply and then in the 30-day waiting period some staff member would tip off my competitor so that he could slide in just under me. This would be serious. And we would have to find an answer.

At bottom, I feel I am talking primarily about material that is out of copyright. If it is out of copyright but still in print, then RRB would have no role to play, except as one or all of the available editions sought the RRB *nihil obstat* to reassure the Association of Research Libraries members that the reprinter was playing ball. There would be no fee to anyone requesting the *nihil obstat* for an edition already in print. On reprints of titles like *Tom Sawyer* the question would never be raised.

One of the assignments of the RRB would be to identify needed reprints. If the work were in copyright, it might approach the copyright owner and present its reasons why he should either reprint himself or license a reprint. If the work were out of copyright, it might put the suggestion before the reprinters it was in touch with, inviting applications for a green light.

The Art of Valuing Old
and Rare Books

How do you tackle your out-of-print problems? The best answer is quite simply to put those problems in the hands of a good o.p. dealer *and make it worth his while*. His problem is earning a living. If you can help him with his problem, he'll help you with yours.

When Arthur A. Houghton, Jr., paid $42,000 for the Shuckburgh copy of the Gutenberg Bible, back in 1953, the price may have represented a perfect equilibrium between supply and demand, as of that moment, all scientifically worked out in the bidding process. The price recently being quoted on this very copy was $2,500,000. I expect the buyer may even later congratulate himself for having got a bargain in case no copy of it ever goes so cheaply again.

Trading in rare books is an art, not a science, and all the practitioners do make their mistakes. When you buy too cheap, that's the dealer's mistake. When you buy too dear, that's your mistake. If there is such a thing as a "right" price for a rare book, then it is the price which neither buyer nor seller will later regret.

Most of us have a gut feeling that an honest merchant shouldn't take too large a markup above his costs. This may be all right for groceries — or in-print books — but it hardly applies to rare books. By this reasoning the junkman who paid a penny a pound for some old newspapers and found among them a copy of the first printing of the constitution of Texas ought to stand ready to sell it for 2 cents!

Any dealer who values your friendship will try not to charge you more than you'd pay elsewhere. But he can never be wholly up to date on this. Furthermore, his pricing will have to cover any special service he may give you. If he puts $10 worth of time into locating a $2 item, he is more deserving of some hard-cash consideration from you than some other dealer whose service does not extend beyond letting you spend your own time scanning his shelves.

Book dealers usually *have* no meaningful "cost" on an item. There's just no way to figure costs when you buy a ton of old books, bring a lifetime of expertise to bear on the problem of which to junk and which to put in the 10-cent bins — and then come up with one rarity.

A book dealer isn't on salary. He may be like everybody else in that his wife will be asking for the household money every week, and the landlord will be asking for the rent every month. But nobody pays *him* on any such schedule. Even a one-man shop operated from an old barn needs to put an average of $100 a day into the cash drawer, rain or shine, summer or winter, or else strike it rich just often enough to balance out the lean periods.

For the likes of you and me, who have always had a paycheck coming in regularly, it is hard to identify with someone for whom nothing is certain but uncertainty. I am not sure, being a city boy myself, but I suspect that dealing in rare books may be somewhat like ranching. You work, and you work, but in the end it makes no never mind what your costs were; you'll get what the market is paying.

The key factors in the pricing of rare books are rarity, demand, and condition. Right now demand is being greatly affected by inflation. Right now your bank deposits are losing value at the rate of 6 percent a year, and if the trend continues, they will lose half their present value in the next ten years. Bonds and stocks aren't doing so well, either. Many investors are reasoning that today's best investment might just be rare books, or coins, or stamps, or works of art, or antiques.

A rare book is worth the quoted price if someone can be found who is willing to pay it. That's the only rule.

Index